"*Detonate* will open your eyes to see the processes, policies, and organizational practices that have outlived their usefulness to customers, employees, and investors. Steve and Geoff give us new ways of operating logically that better align with the fast-changing requirements of our future 'everything is digital' world."

—**Lowell McAdam**,
Chairman and CEO, Verizon Communications

"Tuff and Goldbach build a compelling case for why conventional wisdom and 'best practices' are the surest way to get average results. If you truly aspire for outstanding leadership results, the words you never want to hear are 'that's the way we've always done it.' The authors of this book explain how to 'blow up' practices that companies adopt to reduce risk and, in doing so, renew your business and your organization. A must-read for any business leader!"

—**Chip Bergh**,
President and CEO, Levi Strauss & Co.

"In a fast-changing, disruptive world, *Detonate* provides great insight to how you need to transform the behavior of your organization to innovate and stay competitive. Most organizations are trapped in the pursuit of best practices and risk avoidance. This is a book for leaders."

—**Mark Costa**,
Chairman and CEO, Eastman Chemical Company

"*Detonate* is rooted in the real world of human behavior, unlike so many of the practices that organizations adopt out of risk avoidance and maintain out of shear bureaucratic entropy. Tired of textbook thinking? This book challenges conventional wisdom and provides paradigm-shifting solutions."

—**Tony Ciepiel**,
Chief Operating Officer, Vita-Mix Corporation

"The authors have been helping organizations 'blow up' some of their best practices for a long time. They know what they're talking about because they've seen it. They have been able to boil down successfully what they know into a readable and useful volume."

—**Ofra Strauss**,
Chairperson of the Board, Strauss Group

# Detonate

# Detonate

Why—and How—
Corporations Must
Blow Up Best Practices
(and bring a beginner's mind)
To Survive

GEOFF TUFF
STEVEN GOLDBACH

WILEY

Published by John Wiley & Sons, Inc., Hoboken, New Jersey.
Published simultaneously in Canada.

For general information on our other products and services or for technical support,
please contact our Customer Care Department within the United States at (800)
762–2974, outside the United States at (317) 572–3993 or fax (317) 572–4002.

Wiley publishes in a variety of print and electronic formats and by print-on-demand.
Some material included with standard print versions of this book may not be included
in e-books or in print-on-demand. If this book refers to media such as a CD or DVD
that is not included in the version you purchased, you may download this material at
http://booksupport.wiley.com. For more information about Wiley products, visit
www.wiley.com.

*Library of Congress Cataloging-in-Publication Data is Available*

ISBN 9781119476153 (Hardcover)
ISBN 9781119476115 (ePDF)
ISBN 9781119476177 (ePub)

Cover design: Paul McCarthy

Printed in the United States of America

10  9  8  7  6  5  4  3  2  1

*To our families,*

*Martha, Rider, Quinn, Mason, Hunter, Michelle, and Grayson: Thanks for your patience with us in ways that extend well beyond the project at hand.*

# CONTENTS

# PREFACE

**M**aybe you love your job.

Maybe you hate it.

Either way, at some point, you'll find yourself doing something and thinking, "Why on earth am I doing this; what value can it possibly bring?"

And if you happen to be employed by an established, large business that has proven success in its field with a tried and true model, you likely wonder this with some frequency.

Tens of thousands of people wake up every day to do exactly what the company's forebears did.

Most of the time, people assume that those are just the rules of business by which they must live. If this were just a case of wasted time and some degree of human misery, that would be one thing.

But we believe we have entered an era in which continuing to blindly follow business playbooks may cause an existential threat to the average business.

*Detonate* is our solution to this problem.

# PART I

# LIGHT THE FUSE

# Chapter 1

## *Tinderbox: Hazardous Unwritten Rules*

The two of us grew up watching baseball in the 1970s and 1980s when it was a much different game than it is now. In fact, pretty much since baseball's origin, most managers would use the sacrifice bunt to get a runner from first base to second base with nobody out.

Where did this strategy originate? We're not sure, but our hypothesis lies in baseball's earliest days (pre-1900). Equipment was less robust, and as a result, home runs were rare. Therefore, the possibility of scoring runs in "chunks" through home runs and extra base hits was low. Over time, the choice to bunt developed into conventional wisdom for baseball managers. It became the default, no-thinking option. You just did it. And if you didn't do it, baseball writers would pick apart your decision, and your job would be in jeopardy.

The logic for bunting was that you got a runner into scoring position – second base – where a single could, in theory, allow the runner to score. If you gave up an out, but got the runner to second, you might be in a better position to score. This thinking was pervasive in baseball for most of its history, even in the midst of a fundamental shift in player ability and nature of the game. Eventually, power hitting increased, raising the opportunity cost of a bunt. And a growing emphasis on pitch count – working the number of pitches to force teams to go to their bullpen earlier in the game – ran counter to the reality that bunts are most effective when used early in the count. But still, teams were bunting.[1]

Then, Billy Beane and his team, the Oakland A's, decided to put into practice a concept originated by Bill James: a rejection of the notion that bunting was a good idea. Their logic was that outs were precious. You had only three outs every inning and to give one up – 33% of your capacity – for the *chance* that you might score only one run made little sense. They used statistical analyses to show that bunting would not probabilistically maximize the number of runs you might score. At the time, people panned this concept. But then it started to work and the A's started to win. The Michael Lewis book *Moneyball* has popularized this story; in the eponymous film, Billy Beane (played by Brad Pitt) used it as a metaphor for a bet paying off well.

Why, after 100 years, did a team decide to put this strategy into practice? As is often the case, necessity was the mother of invention. The A's had no money to sign proven players, and Beane realized that following the same strategy as other teams was a recipe for mediocrity at best. He had nothing to lose; nobody expected him to do well if he lost. So he had the necessary preconditions for thinking about the situation and asking, "So, why is that we do it like this?" The answers he got back were various versions of, "This is what we've always done."

When you hear someone say, "This is what we've always done," you know that you're dealing with conventional wisdom – the thinking that governs a habitual decision or choice. People fail to question the logic for this behavior. It simply is the automatic choice – the safe choice. But the problem with actions that take on conventional wisdom arises as you become further and further removed from the original reason for the action, as happened with bunting in baseball during the better part of a century.

The people who make the decision – such as the manager calling the bunt – stop treating that action as a choice and instead treat it as a rule. But there's no rule in baseball that says you have to bunt when you get a runner on first base with no outs. Similarly, there's no rule in baseball that says you should use a closer in the ninth inning (very recently, some managers such as Terry Francona have begun using their "closers" earlier in the game when it appears the game is on the line). Baseball does have a clear set of rules, which, for the most part, have remained the same since the start of the game. A rule book outlines everything that is legal within the framework. Rules define what can and cannot be. All that falls within the rules is completely fair game to try for the purpose of gaining an advantage on your opponent to score more runs, which is the *objective*. Yet, over and over again, we find ourselves bunting – mindlessly falling into rote best practices.

Rules are the governing body for how you pursue your objective. In sports, the rule book defines the boundaries in which the players can compete. In many industries, regulations and laws broadly define what you can and cannot do, but for the most part, as in sports, businesses have a relatively broad mandate. Still, conventional wisdom gets in the way of creativity. Conventional wisdom is what we see as the right thing to do, often without deeply thinking about why we do it. It's what we've always done – the automatic, nonthinking choice.

This is a book about blowing up those best practices that saturate your business before it's too late. The primary purpose of *Detonate* is to help you begin to spot traditional business activities that need to be questioned because of changes in the world today – and then to help you find different ways of doing things. Some of the examples will appear as caricatures of commonplace situations, but we hope that, in painting them starkly – and sometimes comically – they will stand out in your readers' memory in returning to your daily business lives.

Organizations spend countless hours debating how (not whether) they should implement best practices, and they then convince themselves that they can somehow win with their customers because they will have implemented all of them. Actually, the entire concept of best practices, by definition, means that you're doing the same thing as your competition.

The concept of best practice in and by itself does not offend our sensibilities, despite the title of our book. It's the lazy thinking that surrounds them that does. There are some best practices that may have been good when they were developed but are typically reapplied poorly as they travel. There are some best practices that were smart given the context, but when context changes (as it is now for many businesses), we need to abandon the practice because they've turned into a waste of time and money. And there are some practices that we thought were smart, but with experience we find they are not. The common thread is that we need to move from a world where best practices are the rule to best practices are one of several possible tools for solving a problem.

At one point, there was a good case for bunting – as there is for many best practices. The logic for why bunting made sense was unclear and unquestioned. Then it simply became "what we do" – it ossified into a rule, an orthodoxy that couldn't be questioned. (We'll have more to say about the idea of orthodoxy later in this chapter.) And very few managers went back and analyzed why this choice was so automatic. Those who didn't follow were "rule breakers."

But, importantly, they weren't breaking "rules," they were simply breaking with convention. And that can feel like a dangerous move. But that's exactly what we're here to do: to teach you how to find your best practices and blow them up. The corporate world of scaled business can reap tremendous benefits from our lessons, while start-ups and entrepreneurs will also find great value as they learn what to avoid as they themselves scale.

## WHO WE ARE

We draw the content for *Detonate* from our cumulative experience consulting to some of the world's largest and most successful companies for nearly five decades. We see businesses confusing *conventional wisdom* with *rules* all the time. As a result, they've ended up doing things that don't have a clear logic tracing back to a core objective.

We've seen the successes and failures, the celebrations and flameouts, the heights of excitement and the depths of frustration. We know this stuff is real, and we're confident that any reader who has spent time in a large, established organization will see some parts of their company reflected in our observations. Recognition of collective folly is sometimes enough to catalyze change toward a world in which – at a minimum (and to steal a phrase from one of our clients) – we can stop doing the dumb stuff.

We were concerned that our observations were just that – things we had seen in our own experience that might not be as widespread as we thought they were. So to help us make sure that these practices *are* widespread, we initiated a survey of established organizations to understand what they do. As you'll see, we are skeptical of surveys, so ours only focused on the respondents reporting the behaviors of their organizations, not explaining them. We asked respondents at nearly 300 companies questions that were typically along the lines of, "Do you observe Behavior X at your company?" The results of that survey – together with our own experience dealing with conventional wisdom – are at the heart of *Detonate*.

## WHY BEST PRACTICES PERSIST

For millennia, being part of the pack and blending in has been a good strategy for survival. Evolution has created an animal instinct to swarm in order to create selection pressure and predator confusion. "Safety in numbers" makes it hard to catch one animal when there are multiple similar animals nearby. In addition, a large group with a combination of colors and patterns makes it harder to distinguish one animal from another. Meanwhile, multiple eyes looking out for individual safety turns into safety for all, and a little bit of downtime to chill out and relax a bit every once in a while. Herd mentality ran rampant on the African steppes, and it runs rampant in corporate life today.[2]

There's a good reason for it. Consider, for instance, this well-worn phrase: "Nobody ever got fired for buying IBM."

You've heard the axiom *ad nauseam*.

Buying Big Blue isn't itself the problem.

The problem is this: For most cases in business, the oft-repeated advice implies that all of us must make the safe choice to avoid pain. But when you make the safe choice, and when you avoid pain – and when you run with the herd – it's hard, by definition, to stand out from the pack in the eyes of your customers, which in turn, dooms you in the long run. So, what works in the animal community doesn't translate to the business world.

Sure, sometimes safe choices are the right ones to pursue, but increasingly, the concentric circle between safe choices and best choices is getting smaller. Safe choices are those that are defensible to bosses and other powerful stakeholders. People who make safe choices avoid the possible pain of embarrass-ment or the perception of being stupid or – worse – "way out there." Pursuing the conventional wisdom – bunting, buying IBM – is a normal human trait, but one that does us a disservice.

For employees interested in job preservation, the formula for success has been pretty straightforward, too: Learn from those that came before you; follow conventional wisdom and what they have passed on to you; and when a marginal call comes along, take the safe bet. If that bet turns out to be wrong, then who among your superiors – the ones who imparted the conventional wisdom in the first place and probably would have done the same thing – could fault you for your choice? The world has moved slowly and predictably enough that, most of the time, bad calls can be fixed and employees can get on with their careers.

Of course, there's some hyperbole in this, but not much. After all, self-optimization and personal risk management are why conventional wisdom exists. In this case, the thing being optimized – the objective – is the longevity of employment at the personal level and career success more specifically, what we call the survival of "Me Inc." (a theme we'll return to through-out the book). When you layer on top of the personal a need to manage down risk for the corporation and all that it requires, an observable and simple dynamic turns into a systemic tangle of operating procedures.

Conventional wisdom rests on the notion that "the way things are done" is simply in the ether: As company employees, we live, breathe, eat, and act based on an unstated set of rules that "just are." Most of the time, the rules are unspoken and unwritten and they're often learned on the job – from a mentor or from watching what others in your industry or company do. Occasionally, someone captures some of the rules and throws them in a frame to adorn every conference room in the company.

But most of the time, rules are just assumed to be right. It's the corporate version of herd mentality: Follow the flow of the organization and the instinct of those that have come before you, and you're likely not to be picked off for poor per-formance. But try to do things differently and stray a bit from the pack, and you may discover the grass is not actually greener. You are, in fact, dead meat.

Industry dynamics and externalities might shift the rela-tive importance of any of these at different points in time, but all sit at the heart of any corporate mandate. These organi-zational instincts create the corporate equivalent of individual risk mitigation. Like the hapless employee just trying to protect his job, the corporation aims for self-preservation and spews operating procedures and processes and guidelines as the ulti-mate manifestation of conventional wisdom.

## OSSIFICATION OF PLAYBOOKS

Companies' playbooks – the codification of conventional wisdom – need to be completely rewritten. They may have been successful for decades, and we know that you and your colleagues are attached to them. But in light of what most of you are experiencing – pressure against long-standing business models and ways of working as a result of advances in technology – no amount of incremental improvement is going to create the necessary changes. That's why we decided to call this book *Detonate*. Most core business processes based on conventional wisdom or "best practice" have become ossified and overladen with guidelines to the point that they are virtually unrecognizable from their original design and intended purpose.

Consider the case of Six Sigma, which went from being a highly useful practice to, in many places, an ossified rule book that seems absent any real connection to its original objective. The oil embargo of 1973 was a massive wake-up call for US automotive industry leaders, who suddenly saw competition from foreign companies. The Japanese in particular – focused on quality as a competitive platform since World War II – were able to bring to market more fuel-efficient cars, which addressed a sudden shift in customer requirements. Somehow, these machines were less expensive, higher quality, and better aligned with customer requirements than American cars, and a steady loss of share ensued, eventually rippling to impact many corners of American manufacturing.

The science of continuous improvement was nothing new at the time; the concept of fishbone diagrams had been around for decades. But now American manufacturers were students of the Japanese quality system, professionalizing aspects of it and even creating awards for its successful adoption. The introduction of the Malcolm Baldrige National Quality Award in 1987 catalyzed even more fervor for the topic.

Partially intended to celebrate and reward the sharing of best practices, the Baldrige Award virtually guaranteed that people would document, share, and train others in what worked for them. In the same year, Bill Smith at Motorola took quality to a new level by extending the number of acceptable standard deviations from the specification mean from three to six – hence, Six Sigma. This meant that – applied successfully – output would meet specs 99.99% of the time and would result in 0.02 defects per million opportunities.[3]

Motorola was able to realize massive savings by applying Six Sigma, and the concept snowballed: GE, Xerox, and Kodak, among others, started to pay attention. IBM adopted the approach, improved on certain elements of it, and shared it broadly with its suppliers, engineers, and managers. Suddenly, it seemed all the business world could talk about was Cp, CpK, and DMAIC.

In the 1990s, two ex-employees of Motorola founded the Six Sigma Academy and offered accreditation in varying levels of competence in applying tools such as Lean Six Sigma. Borrowing from nomenclature in proficiency at Eastern martial arts, SSA established the notion of Green, Yellow, Black, and Master belts for Six Sigma practicing professionals. The original spirit of continuous improvement and adaptation to customer expectations, however, started to play second fiddle to process adherence and data collection. Today, in many companies, full departments are dedicated to Six Sigma professionals who are available to join project teams to help them stick to the playbook and learn the lessons of three decades of application. Six Sigma is celebrated for its "rigorous, disciplined approach and well-publicized, proven business successes."

But let's not kid ourselves: Employees treat Six Sigma as a set of rules that project teams must mindlessly follow. It's gotten so bad that a network comedy such as *30 Rock* could devote an entire episode, "Retreat to Move Forward," to mocking Six Sigma, calling out the "pillars of the Six Sigma business philosophy – teamwork, insight, brutality, male enhancement, handshakefulness, and play hard." When your best practice tips over into parody, be careful.

By forgetting the core objective and allowing conventional wisdom to harden into fact, many Six Sigma practitioners have lost sight of the room for creativity in its application. Also disappeared is the culture and mindset needed to innovate and adapt to change.

Six Sigma stands out as a particularly well-documented playbook, and one that businesses now routinely caricature. But it is the more general, harder-to-recognize form of conventional wisdom – that which subtly governs almost every action that we take in our business lives – that we believe to be more insidious.

## PLAYBOOKS PRODUCE ORTHODOXY

Orthodoxy – "a belief or way of thinking that is accepted as true or correct" – is the most insidious form of conventional wisdom. Applied to the corporate world at scale and in the face of exponential change, it's massively value-destroying and potentially disastrous.

Rooted in religion, orthodoxy is adherence to a given faith's doctrine. Its appearance in the business world often bears many of the same hallmarks:

- It is passed down from generation to generation either via spoken or written word and is followed diligently since it is considered fundamental to the belief system.

- It tends to be at the heart of the institution's success model – "Why our belief system and moral code is better than others" or "Why our company is better than competitors."

- It is rarely challenged for fear of accusation of heresy by those responsible for propagating it.

- Even in the face of proof that it may be wrong, adherents quickly rationalize away that proof and/or find other reasons to believe.

The difference between religion and business (at least in this context), though, is that while it's hard to find data to prove or disprove the value of an operating principle when the independent variable is an aspect of divinity, results in business are all too measurable.

In business, orthodoxy is simply the accumulation of conventional wisdom over time, and it underlies the rote work and decision-making that happen in the corporate world every day. Most orthodoxies need to be challenged. But not all do: Some are good, necessary, or inconsequential. Some orthodoxies can even evolve into a helpful set of rules, such as codifying safety procedures at an oil refinery or converting accounting practices into financial regulations. And toasting the founder on the company's birthday might be a simple, annual tradition that can stay. These are orthodoxies, but not ones that serve as blinders to innovation or anchors against progress.

As consumers of others' goods and services, we naturally wonder why things are the way they are. Why do grocery stores force shoppers with the largest baskets – and therefore of the most value – to stand in the longest lines? Why do hotels force tired business travelers to wait until the middle of their workday to check in? Why do gas stations force drivers who are trying to quickly pump gas and get back on the road answer dozens of questions about whether they want a car wash, what their zip code is, and whether they want a receipt? Some of these experiences likely have a reasonable root cause, but not all do.

Generally, orthodoxy exists in categories that all relate in some way back to corporate strategy; we tend to have pervasive beliefs that often go unstated and unchallenged. These exist in many areas such as our goals and aspirations, target customers and why they might choose us, our competition, how our industry works, and how we function internally.

Every time you identify a particular orthodoxy, you should research its existence. We recommend a few steps to dig into this in a bit more detail.

1. Ask why you do things this way and try to dig into where it might have started.

2. Imagine life without this orthodoxy; what would be the impact on your company's activities and/or success model?

3. Find people who behave outside the orthodoxy, either at your company or elsewhere.

4.  Identify a business or service that does exactly the opposite of this orthodoxy.

5.  Pinpoint about a place in the world – or a time in history – where this orthodoxy would be impossible.

All of this should provide you with some perspective on the potential fallout of flipping the orthodoxy.

You'll need to do more, however, to create the confidence to go and do something about this orthodoxy at scale. The key, as you will learn throughout this book, is to get out and try – at a "minimally viable" scale – to challenge the orthodoxy. We borrow the phrase "minimally viable" from the world of design and the notion that designers should test prototypes as early in the development cycle as possible.

Act with the lowest burden of proof possible in identifying and thinking through the orthodoxy, and move quickly to design a test to flip it in a controlled setting. "Minimally viable" in the context of prototyping flipped orthodoxies means that you've designed a test that's a reasonable approximation of the potential impact if you take the action at scale, but contained enough that you're not taking on undue risk if your hypothesis is wrong. (We'll explore these in more depth in Chapter 3.)

Business lore is dominated by stories of winners who have faced risk head-on and won. We celebrate companies such as FedEx, Spanx, and ZipCar because their leaders took a stance of gambling it all on their vision. In the case of FedEx, that was quite literally the case in which founder Fred Smith – in the early 1970s – took the company's last $5,000 to bet on blackjack in Las Vegas. He won, taking home $27,000 and enough to get the company back on track. And then there are also the losers who have been too tentative at a critical moment. Blockbuster critically missed the boat on a dirt-cheap Netflix acquisition. In some circles, to "be Kodak'ed" means being far too shortsighted and risk averse to recognize an existential threat. The critical point that might blindside all of us: It is becoming harder and harder to identify, much less quantify, risk.

## THE PLAN

In the rest of Part I, we'll explore why you need to adopt a *Detonate* mindset now. In Chapter 2, we cover the context and conditions that have led us to where we are today and lay the basic argument for why it's so dangerous if we don't take action. We observe the nature of "rules" in business and why some typical playbooks are in place. We explore the nature of change and why some events of the past five years should convince all of us that the future is unlikely to be governed by many lessons from the past. In Chapter 3, we explore the four principles that will help you adopt the *Detonate* mindset.

Then in Part II, "Blow Up Your Playbooks," we dig into seven specific business "normal operating procedures" that we think should be discontinued and replaced with new practices. In discussing their destruction, we provide some critical guiding principles and mindset shifts for breaking out of old, bad habits. Simplistically, these principles largely comprise the *practical* application – for the established business – much of what appears to come naturally to entrepreneurs.

Part III, "Build Something Better," shows how to make adjustments and how to extend these conversations into long-lasting success. While we have deep personal experience, and have collected a fair degree of data for this book, we know we are only scratching the surface of our collective reader base's potential and ultimate knowledge.

After discovering *Detonate*, you'll be able to

- Spot activities and "orthodoxies" that add no value – or even destroy value – and act with confidence to call them into question.

- Bring to your companies new ways of thinking and acting based on lessons from successful companies of *today*, competing effectively in the digital age, rather than lessons from decades ago.

- Identify within your organizations the right places to go and try some new practices without unduly threatening the immediate operating performance of your core business.

- Spread the word and help others discover a new, more fulfilling way of operating.

That's our plan, but ultimately we have an even bigger goal: We hope to catalyze a conversation that broadens over time to encompass others' insights and additional lessons. We'll discuss that in our final chapter.

We are both fundamentally optimistic. While we're purposely trying to call attention to certain pieces of the business sky falling, we are confident that we, as a business community, can make the shift toward a brighter future.

And if we are able to help, we believe we can not only save some businesses – and maybe even some industries – from extinction but also create more rewards along the way.

We just need to start trying.

# CHAPTER 2

# Spark: Acceleration of the Vicious Cycle

B efore we move forward to examine how to blow up your best practices and what new attitudes to adopt, it's worth taking a step back to consider why unknowingly pursuing conventional wisdom has become a path to almost assured failure.

At both the individual and corporate level, the enabling belief for conventional wisdom is anchored in the perception of permanence – the idea that nothing's going to change, or, if it does, that it will change slowly and predictably. And that has been – until recently – a perfectly reasonable belief system. For the vast majority of business history, companies have simply needed to "evolve" to compete effectively. The pace of change has been such that we have only needed gradual adaptation in order to survive; we haven't *really* needed to consider existential threat.

Put simply, most businesses have operated in a state of linear and evolutionary change. That will change, replaced by something that feels much more disruptive and revolutionary. And the average businessperson is devastatingly ill-equipped to face this new world. If you're not feeling a sense of urgency, you should.

The evidence is undeniable that, even in the past five years, the rise of technology and all things digital has fundamentally altered business landscapes and notions of what we have long held to be true. The advancement of technology is making possible the breaking down of long-standing barriers or allowing companies to replicate customer value propositions at fractions of the costs, or creating goods or services that couldn't have existed not so long ago, and the clock speed of this transition is happening fast because of computing power.

Microfactories that leverage additive manufacturing and crowdsourcing allow new players to challenge scale and scope advantages from day one. We can drive radical improvements in efficiency in completely new ways using technologies such as robotic process automation. New business models founded on data proliferation destroy traditional assumptions about what a cost structure and operating system need to look like. And executives are suddenly discovering that the constraints and trade-offs with which they have been grappling are now extinct.

Consider the case of getting a custom-made shirt. Not too long ago, you would have needed to go to a tailor who would take your measurements. The tailor got paid for their expertise. Now, all that time and cost can be replicated by a camera on a smartphone (this is, for instance, the value proposition of the service M Tailor).

The outcome for the consumer is still the same – a custom-made shirt. But the cost has dramatically shifted. This is an example of disruption in practice. It's not that the tailor was doing anything wrong. It's that technology has enabled the ability to replicate (and perhaps augment, if you consider convenience and time for measurement) what they do and at a considerably lower cost.

Or consider the case of a typical retail business. A prototypical business model was to try to create substantial presence within a given footprint to create the likelihood that customers would notice and ultimately visit and purchase from your store. However, advances in technology and forward thinking have given the consumer what they appear to really want – the ability to have nearly endless selection, the convenience of not leaving their house, and good enough delivery times. What was once an advantage has been turned into an Achilles' heel – too much cost deployed against something the consumer no longer values.

We simply can't presume that the future will unfold at the same pace as the past has – this is true not only for our companies and industries but also for the larger macroeconomic context. Consider the story of the steady spread of globalization – the cross-border movement of goods, services, capital, and labor that has been growing for decades. While experts predict the same steady progress in the future, what if "developed" nations don't gradually turn from service-based economies to information-based ones but do so suddenly? What if "emerging" economies skip development stages altogether? What if new technologies such as robotics and artificial intelligence render supply chain professionals obsolete within five years?

But it's not a question of *if* something is going to happen. It's a question of *when*.

To put it even more bluntly: Uber ate the global taxi industry. And you're hoping it won't happen to your business. But it will, and soon.

## THE IMPACT OF EXPONENTIALS

Founded by Ray Kurzweil and Peter Diamandis, Singularity University (SU) has committed itself to understanding the impact of "exponential technologies" on the world around us. We've talked extensively with SU about how exponentials have the potential to radically change the world around us.

Moore's Law and Kurzweil's Law of Accelerating Returns are both fundamental to understanding the nature of exponential change. The former is likely the better known of the two, and it stems from an observation made by Gordon Moore, the cofounder of Fairchild Semiconductor and Intel. In the mid-1960s, he famously predicted that the number of components per integrated circuit would continue to double every year for at least the next decade. History has squabbled a bit about whether 1 year, 2 years, or 18 months was Moore's predicted doubling time frame, but the reality is that, for

50 years, the prediction of exponential growth in transistor count held true.[4]

As we write, Ray Kurzweil is Director of Engineering for Google, although he's more frequently referred to as its "chief futurist." Kurzweil has enjoyed a storied career as an inventor, entrepreneur, author, speaker, and prognosticator. His Law of Accelerating Returns stipulates that: "the rate of progress in any evolutionary learning environment (a system that learns via trial and error over time) increases exponentially. The more advanced a system that improves through iterative learning becomes, the faster it can progress."[5] Both laws helped provide the foundation for SU's core area of research.

Exponential technologies include – among others – augmented reality (AR), virtual reality (VR), artificial intelligence (AI), robotics, digital biology, and data science. What knits them together is that in each, their power and/or speed doubles every year, or their costs drops by half – or both. Because all are powered by an exponential increase in computing capacity, we can assume (and indeed have seen evidence that) they themselves will grow exponentially as well. Spurred in large part by the vision of cofounder Peter Diamandis – among other roles, the founder of the X Prize Foundation – SU sees the opportunity for unparalleled good and advancement to come from exponentials in addressing some of the world's most pressing challenges.

SU posits that "when two or more of these technologies are used in combination to attack a persistent challenge, the possibility of developing a sustainable solution becomes much more likely." This has given rise to the belief in an "abundance mindset" in which no problem exists that can't be addressed by applying exponential technologies and innovation. As Elon

Musk brings to the here-and-now futuristic visions of democratized space travel, hyperloops and fully autonomous vehicles, SU may be on to something, and indeed we all have ever more reason to be hopeful about the future.

We are likewise optimistic but also see the flip side: the possibility for massive disruption of all aspects of legacy business models. As SU has taught us, humans are simply not equipped to process exponential growth or to even imagine how to harness it because we have always lived in – in fact, evolved in – a linear world. One of SU's famous challenges is to imagine taking 30 steps. Thirty linear steps would take you across the room. Thirty exponential steps – in which the distance covered doubles with each step – would take you around Earth 26 times. Because we all innately assume a constant rate of change, we completely underestimate the power of exponentials: power for good but also for disruption.

## THE CHANGING NATURE OF COMPETITIVE ADVANTAGE

Traditional ways of producing competitive advantage are also being overturned. Bruce Greenwald, an economist at Columbia University's Graduate School of Business, has written extensively about the nature of competitive advantage. He argues that there are three categories of advantage: supply, demand, and economies of scale. Supply advantages stem from a company's proprietary access to an input that enables its customer offer. It might be proprietary or preferred access to raw material inputs, intellectual property, technology or any other input. Demand advantage happens when a company has captive or near-captive access to a group of customers. It's stronger than a preference – which can be changed based on competitors out-differentiating a group of customers. And it's far more than "brand preference," as history is littered with brands that are well "liked" or "admired" only to lose customers to an upstart brand. Demand advantages exist when customers are virtually locked in – typically through switching costs, unconscious habitual behavior, or the cost of finding an alternative provider.[6]

Advantages from economies of scale are based on size and scope of operations. Many perform an inappropriate shorthand equating size with scale advantages. That's not necessarily the case. Scale advantages stem from spreading fixed costs over a large base of revenue such that, when revenue grows, the cost per unit decreases. Competing with companies with scale advantages is hard because the advantaged company earns more profit for similar offers, and the scaled players can invest higher profits into better offers, furthering their differentiation.

These general categories of advantage are principles that have stood the test of time and continue to do so.

However, the specific ways one might create supply, demand, and scale advantages *are* changing.

## Supply

Not too long back, if you were a "creative," there were really only a handful of alternatives where you could make a consistent living doing what you loved. The advertising agency industry had consolidated to a small number of players, so if one wanted to be a creative – or hire a creative advertising agency – there were few options outside the big holding companies. There were a few to be sure, but the big agencies enjoyed a supply advantage as a result of having disproportionate access to creative talent.

While this advantage has not completely disappeared, it is coming under increasing pressure because of technology that has made it easier to source creative work from "the crowd" at a dramatically lower cost.

Additionally, new forms of supply advantages have emerged as a result of technology – consider proprietary algorithms that enable value propositions at new technology companies. These are forms of supply advantages that enable capturing value in new and different ways (e.g., Apple Inc.'s recent acquisition of Shazam).

## Demand

We also see evidence of long-standing demand advantages being challenged across all the barriers of switching costs, search costs, and habit. Cloud computing has fundamentally altered the software landscape. In the past, buying a software platform meant being stuck with a lengthy installation process and scheduled upgrade cycles. Once you had the platform installed, you were loath to switch it out for fear of being forced back to preinstallation square one, not to mention the loss of warranty if you ended up realizing that you made the wrong choice. Now, the cloud requires no on-premise installation – suddenly, software providers must compete purely on functionality and experience.

Search costs have fallen dramatically. Consider the general practitioner doctor. If you found a good one, you stuck with her or him for life. Now, companies such as ZocDoc are reducing the cost of searching for a credible alternative, taking the friction out of the system by crowdsourcing information about doctors and making it simple for potential patients to schedule an appointment, check-in, and know whether their insurance is accepted. While the risk of disliking your new GP still exists, it's dramatically reduced.

Habit? Consider the market for many consumer packaged goods. The world of cognitive psychology explains purchasing the same brand over and over again not because you irrationally "love" the brand, but because it has become an unconscious habit, and your brain doesn't even consciously consider alternatives. However, in a world where the weekly shopping trip has been changed by a preference for online purchasing, some brands will invariably find their advantage waning as the context around the habit has changed.

New habits form via new behaviors, which can create new advantages. Think about how frequently you use an app that sits on your home screen, versus all the alternatives that sit in a folder on your fifth or sixth screen. You're more likely to use the home screen app because it's more easily accessible to your brain.

## Scale

Department stores spread the fixed cost of their real estate, inventory, and merchandiser relationships over a large revenue base. And consumers found the convenience of being able to buy multiple types of goods valuable. With a few exceptions, orthodoxy regarding the dominant importance of location, price, and selection meant that many chains were basically able to ignore the shopping experience because of their scale. Online retail, and the ability to buy as effortlessly from the smallest goods purveyor in a category as from the largest, has turned that on its head. Since we open our front doors to find everything we need these days, convenience and experience have significantly challenged traditional scale advantages in retail. Of course, Amazon is proving out a new type of scale advantage, but it's completely different from the advantage enjoyed by the department stores of 50 years ago.

## URGENCY AND THE VICIOUS CYCLE

Yet there's more to it than just "technological disruption is coming for you." If companies like yours were readily adapting to this new world, we could have skipped writing this book. But they're not. Instead, they pursue their conventional wisdom. Still, in today's world best practices create a vicious cycle of behavior that can prove deadly in a rapidly changing environment. Many scaled businesses have been in a self-reinforcing cycle for most of their existence. We're oversimplifying here, but it goes something like this:

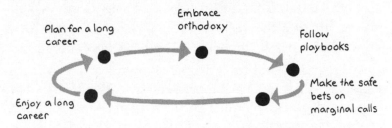

Gradually, processes get further codified, and as employees more stringently apply rules about the right thing to do, more time is wasted. A simple half-day meeting floods its banks to take weeks of work. As employees and their managers get squeezed for time, they adhere even more closely to the playbooks, sometimes acting on blind faith that their sole objective is executing the process. As individual and organizational risk mitigation feed off of each other, acting with blinders on becomes ever more pronounced. And inevitably, burden of proof for almost every decision gradually creeps up: The more data you can bring to a decision, the better the execution of the process step.

The vicious cycle happens when organizational and individual instinct kick in to try to protect the old model in the face of undeniable digital change. Now, it goes something like this:

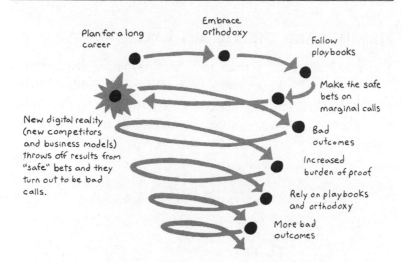

Corporations have become devastatingly inward-focused, structuring and optimizing for process adherence and execution rather than for making *good* choices. This is incredibly dangerous in today's world. This vicious cycle is now accelerating given the increasing clock speed of technological advances that ripple through business systems and the nature of opportunity that they create.

We know one thing for sure: *No* transitions will happen at the same, measured pace that governed shifts in the past. Incremental change will give way to disruptive and even exponential change, and we see proof of it starting to happen already. Barriers to economic efficiency will fall faster than they ever have before, underpinned by enabling technologies and information flow, which are already on an accelerating curve of change.

## RETHINKING THE "GOLDEN RATIO"

All of this has caused us to rethink some of our fundamental research on how innovation works.

In 2012, Geoff coauthored an article in the *Harvard Business Review* about what a well-balanced innovation portfolio should look like. Two important concepts were introduced. First, an innovation portfolio can be characterized well by something we called the "innovation ambition matrix" and a balanced innovation portfolio for a diversified company was characterized by a "Golden Ratio."[7]

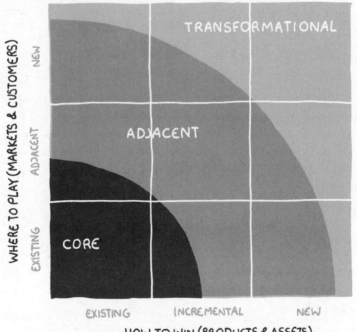

The idea behind the ambition matrix is that innovation, which we defined as the "creation of new economic value," can be framed as a combination of the stuff you use to create new value and the markets and customers you are serving. More formally, we labeled those "How to Win" (the stuff – assets, capabilities, know-how, operating model, etc.) on the *x*-axis and "Where to Play" on the *y*-axis. Each axis has three parts – essentially existing, adjacent, and brand new – and we proscribed two arcs on the matrix to define three levels of ambition for innovation:

1. **Core:** The optimization of existing products and services to serve current customers, sometimes slightly extending the assets to other customers who have similar needs but have been just outside a company's focus until now. This is the foundation of what most well-run businesses are able to do effectively every day.

2. **Adjacent:** Stretching from a position of strength today, either by leveraging customer relationships to offer new types of value or by leveraging an asset base and core capability to stretch into further adjacent customer groups – and sometimes doing both simultaneously.

3. **Transformational:** Deploying new assets and capital to discover new market needs before customers even recognize they have them (note that the "new" row on the Where to Play axis is new to the world, not to the company).

We also discovered that, on average, a well-balanced innovation portfolio was characterized by spending 70% of your time and money on innovation in the Core, 20% in Adjacent, and 10% in Transformational. Importantly, the 70/20/10 ratio is only an average and needs to be customized for any particular business given the specific context of their industry, relative competitive position, and degree of risk tolerance, among other factors. Our intention with the article was to trigger a strategic dialogue about the right balance, not create a new, unintended orthodoxy.

We also discovered two strong tendencies of established companies through our innovation discussions with teams. First, no one – not even the most financially buttoned-up firms – really has a clue where their innovation spend is today. You can go around the table of executives at most companies and ask them to guess the distribution across Core/Adjacent/Transformational and you'll get wildly varying answers. The reality is that most companies just don't have the systems in place to accurately track spend and activity against innovation in all the areas where it occurs.

The other discovery was that everyone vastly overesti-mates the degree to which they are innovating beyond the Core. Even the companies that are most discouraged by their ability to be ambitious with innovation typically guess that they have at least 10–15% of their spend in the Adjacent and

Transformational spaces. But when they have asked us to audit actual spend and activity (usually no small feat), the truth is far more stark.

Typically, we find that more than 90% – and usually more than 95% – of innovation is focused on the Core. Why? The simplest summary of myriad answers is that the Core is an easy place to hide. Sometimes it's a series of pet projects that have languished in the lab for years as their engineers wait for nights-and-weekends time to continue their work. Sometimes it's a collection of one-off requests from "really important customers" that have been pushed and justified by Sales because "if we don't deliver that one-off, the rest of the base business from that customer will be at risk." Sometimes it's the result of a company-wide contest to "collaborate" via an ideation platform, leaving the contest owners with months of work to sort through ideas and give each its due lest they alienate the contributors.

This waste is enabled by an orthodoxy that we'll explore further later on in the book – that filling the "front end of inno-vation" – the idea generation phase – will lead to value creation because more ideas *must* produce something that sticks. In real-ity, what it creates is a logjam and a money pit sifting through too many ideas with minimal potential. The work of the inno-vation team becomes process management instead of actually creating new ideas that delight customers. And because people tend to brainstorm about things they know, most of the ideas tend to be about the core business and hold little promise for creating high returns.

All of this waste would be simply disheartening in a world in which companies have the time to unwind their clogged innovation systems, to shut down some spend in the Core, and to redirect it to higher ambition activities. But because advances in technology are creating discontinuity in business models, there is no longer the luxury of time; it's now an existential threat. And the Golden Ratio is likely more along the lines of 50/30/20 as a result of this discontinuity in core businesses.

## From the Known to the Unknowable

In the face of the kind of radical change that we've documented in this chapter, a dangerous dynamic starts to emerge that can be understood by looking at the innovation ambition matrix in a simpler way:

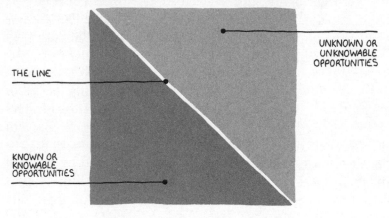

**AMBITION MATRIX REIMAGINED**

UNKNOWN OR
UNKNOWABLE
OPPORTUNITIES

THE LINE

KNOWN OR
KNOWABLE
OPPORTUNITIES

We have drawn a diagonal intersect from top left to bottom right of the matrix, which describes two different domains of opportunity for companies as they set out to innovate. Below the intersect is a space that can be thought of as the "known or knowable" opportunity set. These are markets in which we play in today and/or markets and customers who – if we don't serve them – we can access via traditional market research methods. We can ask them questions to understand what they need, how strong that need is, what it would take to change their behavior, and how much of something they would be willing to buy at various price points and can be sure that the responses we get back will be reasonably accurate and believable. That's because we can all talk about solutions that either exist in the market today or are close enough to what exists that it doesn't take an extreme act of imagination to understand what we're talking about.

Above the line is a completely different ball game. This is the unknown and – in some cases, unknowable – domain of opportunity. The very far adjacent and transformational spaces are ones that the average company hasn't played in before and for which there have been few, if any, solutions imagined by anyone in the past. Given that the "new" market and customer needs row is about anticipating needs before anyone is able to express them, we can be sure that that is untrodden ground. Steve Jobs famously said: "It's really hard to design products by focus groups. A lot of times, people don't know what they want until you show it to them."[8] Given the long-standing success of Apple at surprising and thrilling the world with its new product launches, it's clear Jobs was one of the few who learned how to institutionalize playing in this "above the line" space. But most don't get it right – and in fact end up destroying value when they try to play there.

Almost 100 years ago, the University of Chicago economist Frank Knight popularized, at least within business and economic circles, the notion of the difference between uncertainty and risk – our above and below the line. "Uncertainty must be taken in a sense radically distinct from the familiar notion of Risk, from which it has never been properly separated," he wrote. "The essential fact is that 'risk' means in some cases a quantity susceptible of measurement, while at other times it is something distinctly not of this character; and there are far-reaching and crucial differences in the bearings of the phenomena depending on which of the two is really present and operating. It will appear that a measurable uncertainty, or 'risk' proper, as we shall use the term, is so far different from an unmeasurable one that it is not in effect an uncertainty at all."[9]

In other words, in Knight's formulation, risk is measurable and manageable; uncertainty is not. While we live in a world that others frequently characterize as volatile and uncertain, we would say that there are things that are becoming more uncertain, but there are also things that are migrating from uncertainty to risk. We would certainly concede the point that we are seeing increasing levels of uncertainty as it relates to technological advancement, geopolitical instability (relative to the last 30 years), and cybersecurity. That being said, because of the same technological advances, many things that were once unknowable are now knowable. For instance, we now can better predict customer response rates thanks to more advanced behavioral models. Further, we can also measure and monitor behavior more accurately and at scale due to sensor technology leveraging the Internet of Things. So we aren't necessarily only seeing a shift in a single direction.

Of course, if you can measure it, you can manage it – to twist the adage apparently falsely attributed to Lord Kelvin.[10] Many of the playbooks that we see in place today come from managing this risk.

Innovation opportunities that exist "below the line" are ones with inherent risk. For some, the risk is extremely low, and for others – as you approach that diagonal intersect – it's a bit higher, but it is by definition measurable.

The core issue is that most companies try to deploy a single innovation system to play across the entire ambition matrix and that just doesn't work. The job of managing innovations "below the line," when you can work with valid data and reasonable hypotheses based on direct experience, is completely different from work "above the line," where you actually need to ignore what customers say and proceed with extreme skepticism when someone claims to understand the opportunities and most important trends impacting that space. We devote a good portion of this book – particularly in Part II – to writing about practices that need to change once you start to work in the world of the unknown and unknowable.

Once you cross the diagonal intersect and start playing in far adjacent and transformational spaces, where lack of easily available data makes risk immeasurable, there is genuine uncertainty that cannot be "managed down." So when companies apply traditional risk management systems and playbooks to try to control uncertainty, bad things happen.

## LESSONS FOR THE FUTURE

This all matters only because we have crossed a threshold in terms of where the balance of opportunity lies for most companies. In a world dictated by an average "right" balance of 70/20/10, basic arithmetic would suggest that roughly 80% of innovation opportunity lies "below the line," if risk can be managed down. In a world where the necessary balance has shifted to 50/30/20 and continues to head in that direction, we find ourselves looking at almost half of our opportunity and the vast majority (and growing) of future return governed by uncertainty. In the past, when change was mainly linear in nature, we had time and tools to manage risk and course correct as necessary; there was lots of leeway for mistakes. Now, as we experience exponential change, any attempt to apply risk management tools and process methodically could prove disastrous.

We can't presume that the pace of change will stay constant and that the lessons from the past will help us in the future. In fact, we must presume the opposite. Histories covering national economic development or supply chain management or any other business topic should be treated as histories and nothing more. And to take it one step further, we believe we actually need to unlearn the lessons that have helped us in the past.

Hence, the logic behind *Detonate*.

## CHAPTER 3

# Coordinates: Targeting the Blast

In the early twentieth century, the venerable and growing Sears, Roebuck and Company needed to expand its operations outside of Chicago, and chose northeast Philadelphia as one of its key locations. Between 1918 and 1920, more than 2,000 workers built the Sears Merchandising Center: a nine-story, 2.7-million-square-foot mammoth of a building. Many who grew up in the area considered the Center a key landmark of the city and a central part of their lives, with its 14-story clock tower solidly marking the passage of time from decade to decade for the better part of that century.

On October 31, 1994, seven seconds and 12,000 pounds of explosive was all it took to bring the Philadelphia Sears Tower down. That event still holds the world record for the largest explosively demolished building.[11]

Our psyches typically relate explosions with a bad event: a bomb being dropped during wartime, a terrorist deploying a suicide vest, an accident at a plant. But detonations have also played a critical role in enabling progress. When it's impossible to sufficiently repair old infrastructure, we may need to blow up a bridge to make way for one that will be stable for longer. When history and memory are anchors to progress, we may need to tear down monuments to allow the collective to move forward.

When the vision for a future is not simply derivative of the past, we may need to reduce a stadium to rubble to allow for a new, technologically advanced one that dramatically improves sports fans' experience. As in the demise of the Sears Merchandising Center, how we do this to avoid collateral damage is critically important and requires deep expertise.

In the world of controlled demolition, building implosion is "the strategic placing of explosive material and timing of its detonation so that a structure collapses on itself in a matter of seconds, minimizing the physical damage to its immediate surroundings." This is true of blowing up business processes, too. Where we start is a strategic choice. When we make the move could impact how broadly it will be noticed and what the knock-on effects will be. We want the collapse to be instantaneous and controlled, recognizing that we may very well want to keep intact immediately adjacent activities or systems.[12]

So, where to start? If we were to target for destruction any business process that feels like wasted time, we'd likely end up with a long list. Indeed, when "asked around" – unscientifically via social media – to help us ideate what processes people really think add no value to their businesses, we got a comprehensive array of (often humorous) responses:

- "Risk management procedures that don't actually manage risk."

- "Long slide deck-making for internal audiences!"

- "A desire to satisfy the 'cult of collaboration' in which all opinions are equal and everyone can be creative."

- "Getting caught up in tracking process against internal targets believing that driving the process will deliver the results . . . which just creates a diversion from actually delivering the results."

- "When 'Jimmy from Finance' has an idea about marketing, and it has to get vetted if we are 'being collaborative,' just slowing everything down."

- "Rollover budgeting practices (e.g., prior-year budget plus 4%) that carry dead weight investing year over year."

The list goes on. But some of the themes that came up time and time again are indeed related to the playbooks that need to go.

Broadly, there are seven corporate mainstays that we challenge in depth in the next part of the book. At a headline level, though, the arguments can be summarized in a sentence each. **Financial Forecasting and Budgeting** too often optimizes for a spreadsheet outcome rather than a coherent business outcome end goal rather than a desired business outcome. The underlying purpose of **Strategic Planning** gets lost as the process becomes templatized and routinized around an annual calendar. **Syndicated Data** gives us insights that are readily available to our competitors and fools us into thinking we have an advantage. **Traditional Insight Generation** relies too much on syndicated data, irrelevant "expert" insight, and information that is prone to self-reporting bias. Most **Risk Management Systems** – and in particular Stage-Gate systems – have lost sight of their purpose in favor of process adherence. Somehow along the way some crazy notions about not just risk tolerance but **Celebrating Failure** have taken root. And finally, **Org Charts and Career Paths** have created the perception of permanence – one of the critical enablers of orthodoxy.

Not every one of these is flawed absolutely, and each one is rooted in a good idea at one point in time. But collectively, they encompass the vast majority of the business "best practice" that must be taken apart to break the vicious cycle.

That's how we'll approach Part II. We turn our attention to breaking down existing processes businesses use and apply some of the principles we think companies will need to employ to succeed in the future. We'll demonstrate why many common practices today simply don't make sense and how you can apply our core *Detonate* principles to make it more likely the process will contribute to marketplace success.

But most companies don't have the luxury of throwing everything out the window. They have customers to serve today and shareholders who expect them to exceed expectations and maybe even kick out a dividend every now and then. One option in the face of that reality is the equivalent of the organizational "oh well" shrug, wishing you could "play start-up" but steering clear for fear of catastrophic failure. Whether we like it or not, though, the chances of catastrophic failure because of *not* doing anything are pretty high already and likely rising. The average life span of a company listed in the S&P 500 in the early 1960s was right around 60 years. Today, it's under 20.[13]

So, instead, we strongly encourage tossing the "all or nothing" thinking out. It's not a question of *whether* to try on some of the principles and enable the detonation, but of *where to start* and *to what extent*. In managing the business of today – the so-called below-the-line space – most companies are not going to want to dramatically change every process they have in place. But they absolutely should empower anyone involved in the business to challenge orthodoxy and ask why things are done the way they are. In managing the business of tomorrow, "above the line" options should abound. The trick is to avoid presuming that the same rules apply and that legacy assets and business systems must be considered, and to instead cherry-pick the benefits of being a scaled business (customers, capital, breadth of operations, etc.) and combine them with the *Detonate* mindset to create advantage and just maybe beat a bunch of start-ups at their own game.

## THE *DETONATE* PRINCIPLES

Four principles create the basis for this transformation. Anchored in philosophy and work approach rather than processes and playbooks, these core principles to compete effectively in a time of accelerating change are:

1. Focus your activities on understanding and driving **human behavior**

2. Bring a **"beginner's mind"** to all that you do

3. Embrace **impermanence**

4. Build **minimally viable moves** to test and learn

## Human behavior

Think of every strategic plan that didn't work out as planned. And think of where – specifically – it went wrong. Our guess is that when you picture these in your mind's eye, there were two possible reasons. First, there's the story we often hear about *a great strategy that we couldn't execute*. This is where the answer was just so perfect, but the organization couldn't figure out how to create the change necessary so that everyone could behave consistently with the strategy. The second one is *customers didn't respond*, where you launch a new offer, rebrand, or reposition yourself but those customers just don't do what they said they were going to do in some survey.

When we spend time with executives from mostly large Fortune 500 organizations, we generally hear desires to broadly achieve two objectives: *growth* (i.e., they would like to drive higher revenue and profit for the organization), or *transformation*, which usually requires a more company-specific definition, but we'll define here as getting an organization to be able to become something different in the future, presumably with more relevant capabilities for its environment. Although the connection isn't always made clear, these two objectives are based on the premise that achieving them will drive some sort of long-term value creation for the owners of the business or for society in general.

The challenge we see is that most companies have lost sight of the fundamental *subatomic element* of business – changing human behavior. If the objective is to grow revenue or profit, or create new capabilities to transform an organization, then as you peel back the layers of what that will take, you always find yourself requiring a human being to *do something different than what they're doing today*.

" ... requires human beings to do something
they are not doing today."

Achieving revenue growth requires customers to behave differently. Whether it is your current customers paying more for the products or services they are buying today or buying more frequently, customers of your competition switching to your offer, or new customers entering your category, growing your revenue, at the end of the day requires human beings to do something they are not doing today.

The same principle can be applied within your organization for the purpose of transformation – both large scale (e.g., digitalizing the business model) and smaller scale (e.g., shifting operations to drive out cost). Building new capabilities or broadly getting an organization to act differently requires human beings to change their behavior – whether it be to perform new tasks, make different choices, work faster or slower, work with different people, or collaborate more or less.

There is literally an unlimited number of possible new or different human behaviors that can support a broad organizational transformation.

For both growth and transformation, changing human behavior requires motivation to do something different. For revenue growth, we believe that changing human behavior should be the driving force behind all marketing organizations. What will cause customers to behave differently than they are today? And every broad organizational transformation requires understanding how it will get its people to act differently. What new training is required? What new management systems (e.g., operating models, incentives and measures, cultural change) are required to get people to act in the manner consistent with the transformation?

## Beginner's mind

Anyone who has been – or been anywhere close to – an entrepreneur will recognize this principle as fundamental to the start-up world. And in many ways, a lot of the prevailing mindset in the corporate world that leads us into the vicious cycle could use a jolt from start-up thinking. No entrepreneur presumes that employment is permanent or that they will never go out of business. Most approach opportunities as if the only way they will win is to actually *ignore* the way things have been done in the past. Start-ups generally look for shortcuts and the most efficient means possible to achieve a singular goal.

If you have grown up within a company or an industry, then you can likely claim to be some degree of expert: in how you do things, in how your competitors are likely to react in certain situations, in what your suppliers try to do with their prices at the end of a quarter, in how open regulators are to certain types of mergers, in what motivates your employees.

If change is slow and linear, and past strong performance is a great predictor of future success, you will be wise. If new competitors are suddenly showing up on the scene completely unpredictably, and new technologies appear at your disposal for various purposes in dizzying frequency, your wisdom is actually not just useless but possibly dangerous.

The people best at spotting orthodoxy are often those newest to a company or industry and those most often found asking: "Huh! I wonder why they do it that way?" Many students of the modern business world know the concept of bringing a "beginner's mind" from the likes of Steve Jobs or Marc Benioff, who, as two of the most successful CEOs and visionaries of the digital era, believed in the power of curiosity.

"In the beginner's mind there are many possibilities, but in the expert's there are few." So begins Shunryu Suzuki's classic *Zen Mind, Beginner's Mind*. Yes, these words were aimed at those learning to effectively practice Zen Buddhism, not for our readers learning how to avoid screwing up their company. But we love Suzuki's opening line for how true it holds in the business world. The beginner's mind is also core to recognizing orthodoxy.

Innovation lore is littered with stories of brilliant minds coming to disrupt industry norms by seeing past those who are, ironically, limited by their expertise. Watch industry stalwarts never imagined that Apple could dominate because they "knew" that watches were as much about style, self-actualization, and engineering marvel as they were about telling time; why else would people for decades be willing to spend many tens of thousands of dollars for some brands? And then in September 2017, the Apple Watch became the top-selling watch brand in the world just two years after its launch and five years after the invention of the "smart watch" category with Pebble. Jony Ive and his team at Apple didn't set out to create a better watch. They started with the connected insights that technology was moving onto the body and phones were ruining peoples' lives as a constant attachment and distraction. They designed the Apple Watch to enable connection and to "provide it in a way that's a little more human, a little more in the moment when you're with somebody."[14]

Meanwhile, auto executives "knew" that once cars came off the production line, the only way to improve them was to get them back into a shop for upgrading or retrofitting – a tremendously expensive undertaking. So it was critical to get the manufacturing right the first time and to pack as much of the latest technology into a car as possible. There was no way out of this process. And then along came Elon Musk and Tesla who taught us that cars can be upgraded and updated via software. By March 2016, demand for the Tesla Model 3 was unlike anything the automobile industry had ever seen before – more than 325,000 reservations, it claimed, within a week of the announcement. Musk had set out to reinvent the automobile manufacturing process at the same time that he acted on his belief that electric and autonomous vehicles would grow exponentially.[15] The company has – so far – blown orthodoxy out of the water, constantly thrilling customers with overnight software releases such as the "Insane Mode" for acceleration. While Tesla is still working through production challenges as we write, Musk has changed the world of cars for good.

For decades, retailers "knew" that the key to success was a combination of great real estate, strategic merchandising, and effective and engaging in-store promotion. And they also "knew" that you needed to demonstrate economic viability and growing profitability to get investors to stick with you. And then along came Jeff Bezos and Amazon.

As these and many other examples show, entrepreneurs navigate the world of uncertainty with success when they have an absence of prior habits and belief systems. This enables them to apply first principles to most directly serve customer needs and to focus primarily on driving the behavior for success.

But here's the key. Even though we can be obsessed with innovative start-ups that shake established industries, the power of a beginner's mind is not limited to new companies. Consider the case of IBM: a company that has been successful in systematically challenging orthodoxy across at least two different CEO transitions. When Lou Gerstner took the helm in 1993, the company had ridden a roller coaster of performance from a peak a decade before to a recent, deep valley. One insider put it succinctly: "IBM was at the pinnacle of success. Over the previous two decades we had practically invented general-purpose computing for business. By 1984 we were the toast of Wall Street. Less than a decade later, we were toast. In 1993 we posted what at the time was the biggest loss in the history of corporate America, $8 billion. We had missed a number of key technology shifts. Customers who had previously said 'no one ever got fired for buying IBM' were abandoning us for faster, more nimble competitors."[16]

IBM had long prided itself on its culture of innovation and – perhaps because of the complacency that comes from knowing that you are always the "safe choice" for customers – a promise of lifetime employment. With a culture of "Think," IBM employees enjoyed a fairly long leash for how they spent their time. But Gerstner's game was fiscal responsibility. By focusing on financial targets, holding managers accountable for meeting them, and firing them if they didn't, Gerstner immediately threw orthodoxy and complacency out the window. Though layoffs may not have endeared him to many inside the company, they did send a very clear signal that the old playbooks and assumptions didn't apply anymore and likely allowed other business moves – such as eliminating some products, establishing new categories, and bundling products to solve business problems – to take hold much more efficiently.

Gerstner's management system soon took on orthodoxy of its own. After a decade under his leadership, IBM had four major businesses: hardware, software, services, and PCs. A corporate executive committee (the CEC) oversaw the company, including the leaders of the businesses and core corporate functions. This model worked for a company that saw as its strategic mandate to provide enterprise solutions to businesses in 170 countries, operating as a single, globally integrated entity. The company could easily have rested on its laurels and business model and become entrenched.

But in the past 15 years, two more CEOs have come on the scene and shaken things up. First, Sam Palmisano blew up the CEC – a "council of barons" – anticipating "a world in which trillions of bits of information generated by everyone everywhere had to be analyzed so that it could be used to solve problems facing modern business and governments everywhere."[17] This required more agility and less centralized decision-making in order to be responsive to rapidly shifting customer needs. And it also required divestment of two lower-margin heritage businesses that seemed strategically critical and central to the IBM image: PCs and hardware.

Perhaps emboldened by improving performance, Palmisano predicted in 2010 that IBM would roughly double its EPS within five years. When Ginni Romety took over in 2012, she soon realized that meeting that goal could end up preventing IBM from being able to reinvent itself yet again. So she took the personal risk to back away from the plan just two years into her tenure. Since then, Romety has been on a mission to turn IBM in to a cloud-based solutions business, making bold investment and divestment moves along the way. While Romety is still writing her part of the IBM book (and recent declining performance may foreshadow that this chapter may not end well), it's clear is that she has followed in the footsteps of her forbears in challenging conventional wisdom for success.

The key in this story is that unlike Billy Beane of the Oakland A's, none of these leaders were working from a starting place of a demonstrably failing model. Each was willing to question orthodoxy well before warning sirens were wailing, taking on significant personal and reputational risks. They collectively built a culture of constant transformation and of challenging the way things have been done in the past. As Romety put it, "It doesn't matter if you're an insider so long as you don't try to protect the past."[18] We see the reluctance to challenge orthodoxy frequently in the corporate world today, and it only gets worse going down most org charts.

## Embracing impermanence

In traditional business training, the mindset of permanence is deep. As we've discussed in Chapter 2, until recently this was a reasonable position to hold. In researching this book, we explored the genesis stories of business processes and started seeing time and time again a gradual and uninterruptable reflection of historical development. It seems as though even our most revered business theorists and historians have a development story defined by a state of constant progress that will continue on indefinitely. This is true in both the straightforward stories of business process and in the more abstracted stories about macroeconomic development.

In the same way, the archetypal corporation believes that it will never go out of business. For many years, for many people, for many companies: Basically true. From the early 1900s until just a few years ago, the business models needed to compete – along with assumptions about industry structure – were predictable and stable. Early last century, you gained advantage through scale or scope and, once you had that, you just needed to drive operational excellence to continuously improve performance. A bit later, the strategists came along and taught us all that differentiation mattered. We recognized that there were natural constraints around how differentiation was achieved and that we had to make trade-offs among, for example, cost, convenience, and functionality. Sure, we had to compete but that presupposed that if we did a basically good job, we'd be around to compete indefinitely.

Much the same is true of employees. While most employees don't really believe that employment could still be for life, many still *act* like it is.

No more. If we truly want to embrace the mindset that we need to *Detonate* our playbooks, we have to embrace the idea that impermanence reigns at all levels: At the personal level, none of us is employed for life, and we have to be prepared to create our own careers and pursue opportunities. At the other end of the scale – the macroeconomy – instead of witnessing the straight-line development of nations following well-worn paths, we'll see frontier economies moving in directions we never expected, leapfrogging developed economies in new and surprising ways – from the rise of mobile-first economies in sub-Saharan Africa to the rise of new capitalisms in China.

But most relevant to *Detonate* is the idea that we have to be prepared to create structures, processes, and systems that aren't expected last forever.

## Minimally viable moves

Imagine two people who, through some bizarre circumstance, find themselves suddenly walking through an unfamiliar, heavily wooded forest on a dark night. Person A, confident in his athleticism and keen sense of direction, takes long strides forward in an attempt to get out of the forest as quickly as possible. He's okay for the first few steps, but on his fourth, he trips over a log. While stumbling headlong forward, he lands on a mossy rock, and as he swings his arms out wide to avoid toppling over, he exposes his face to sharp tree branch.

Ouch: failure.

Person B, on the other hand, is equally keen to get out of the woods but quickly recognizes that all her prowess on the running track is of no use in a dark forest. She carefully inches one foot forward at a time, pushing into the dark with her toes until she meets some resistance, at which point she puts down that foot and starts with the next. Her progress is a bit meandering, but it is always forward, and she learns along the way to stretch each footstep to its maximum potential. Moving slowly, she learns the pattern of the forest floor; if she bumps up against the log, she doesn't end up in the hospital but readjusts on the go. And as the patterns begin to become second nature, she can tune her attention to a wider array of stimuli that help her navigate toward civilization yet again. She exits the woods not knowing (and never knowing) whether she landed on the most direct route. But it was a good route and ultimately a successful one full of learning and constant course correction. And she makes it out of the uncertain woods quicker, with more intact than her unfortunate friend.

The lesson here is that the single best way to avoid failure is to make sure that every time you make a move in a space governed by uncertainty, that move is open to course correction immediately if it turns out to be a bad one. And ideally, you will learn just a little every time you make a move so that not only do you avoid failing outright but you also build a base of knowledge that allows you operate even more effectively in analogous situations in the future. This is simply an extension of the notion commonly used in design-driven approaches to innovation: the "agile" use of repeated cycles of fast prototyping of a minimally viable offering (MVO). At the heart of this approach is a commitment to build a little, learn a little, build a little more, and so on, until a complete solution is in place. At no point along the way do you take such a big step that failure is a possibility. And at the end of the journey, while you may not know if the resultant solution is the best one, you know it's a good one that gives some degree of success.

We call our slightly expanded version the Minimally Viable Move (MVM), and we see its application in almost any business activity that is done in the face of uncertainty.

A colleague of ours by the name of John Seely Brown – "JSB" in Silicon Valley lore – introduced us to the MVM. Most know JSB as the Chief Scientist of Xerox and Director of the Palo Alto Research Center in the 1990s. He has sat on a variety of boards of famously innovative companies such as Corning and Amazon and has been one of the pioneering researchers in computers and all things digital for the past 50 years. Recently, we took part in a discussion between JSB and a roomful of executives of one of the world's biggest companies. How could we turn this massive tanker of an organization just a little in order to compete more effectively in the digital age? Someone asked JSB what he had learned from his early years of computer research that would help take risks and thrive in the face of the unknown. He got a wide smile on his face and a look of incredulity and said something along the lines of, "You gotta understand, we didn't think of it as taking risks. We were just tinkering. We'd try something and if it worked, great; if it didn't you'd try something else. We never saw anything we were doing as having failed because we were always just trying to learn and to make something that didn't work great work better. We all grew up as tinkerers!"

Unfortunately, most of the corporate world doesn't tinker. People learn through apprenticeship to work toward mastery and take on additional responsibility only when they've proved to their mentors that they can replicate their approaches. Naturally, the danger is that what constituted mastery in the past might be irrelevant in the future. With technological advances impacting an increasing proportion of the economy, masters can't afford *not* to tinker to ensure their skills remain competitive. Making minimally viable moves to constantly work toward something better is a great way to advance.

We want to apply this principle to the broad field of risk management. To be sure, it's a vital function for organizations today. Risks are real, and companies must put meaningful controls in place to ensure the survival of the organization. Cybersecurity and similar requests require care, attention, and advance planning because how organizations respond to security breaches is as, if not more, important than preventing them in the first place.

But we're delving into business risk in the context of a changing world. When we talk to people about the challenges of risk management systems, we hear several broad kinds of complaints usually falling into the categories of being slow, cumbersome, and, at the end of the day, not really capturing the risk.

Our observation is that organizations often get confused between the concepts of being in control and managing risk. Companies like to be in control as much as possible. But the desire to *feel* in control is substituted for *actually being in control*, if you define being in control as being able to meaningfully impact the outcome. Lots of processes and systems surrounding a new innovation or a new strategy sure do give managers the feeling of being in control – "We did all this work; don't we feel good?" But more work doesn't always create a smaller range of possible outcomes in the real world – the definition of reducing risk.

In Part II, we'll examine two failure modes in risk management that are closely tied to the idea of minimally viable moves. First, there's the trouble with applying a one-sized-fits-all approach to new-offer development, typically a "phase-gate" system. Risk comes in different flavors, and applying the same process to different problems doesn't work much of the time. Typically, the outcome is slowing down ideas that can't be better managed except by putting something in the market and seeing how the world responds.

The second failure mode is the opposite. Companies come under pressure to "make a bold move" and put something out in the world that is way more of an investment than necessary to initially see if the idea had merit. And when it ultimately fails, leadership puts on a brave face and suggests the failure should be celebrated.

Neither of these failures is necessary if we apply the principle of minimally viable moves. If it's a knowable and predictable challenge, then we should apply all the resources necessary to manage risk down to an economically attractive level. Here, classic risk management systems work well. But when new challenges arise, applying tools that were designed for past issues fails, giving way to trial and error. You just have to make it so that if there is an "error" it doesn't hurt much – like running directly into a mossy rock and scraping your face on a tree branch.

If you want to see minimally viable moves in action, consider the success of what's known as "maker culture," a contemporary community driven by self-described innovators and entrepreneurs who combine a do-it-yourself drive with an enthusiasm for sharing knowledge to "make" offerings for the world. Makers adopt (and, in some instances, create) the latest technologies and innovations to create or hack in the spirit of building better products. The maker movement has evolved into a brand characterized by a culture of democracy, cooperation, sharing, and building. The platforms for learning, sharing, and selling employed by the maker movement are leading to new possibilities for innovation in products, materials, and business models.[19]

Some companies have already yielded success from the maker mentality. Square, now a billion-dollar business, started in a San Francisco open-sourced tool shop when cofounder Jim McKelvey spent one month building the prototype card reader that started the payment start-up's success. Facebook's former motto – "move fast and break things" – embodied the maker culture and was applied across the entire organization. It explained the culture and management style that encouraged employees to keep pushing Facebook products forward, even when users are perfectly fine with the status quo.[20]

As this return to tinkering becomes more prominent within businesses, it gives us the opportunity to revisit existing ways companies "move" innovation forward.

## THE PLAN FOR PART II

In Part II, we'll approach seven different kinds of playbooks – one per chapter – and show how you can target them for demolition. We'll use the four principles that we've explored here – a richer understanding of human behavior, a beginner's mind, embracing impermanence, and using minimally viable moves – to show you how to do it.

We start with "Dismantle Your P&L," where we suggest that focusing on revenue as the output, rather than behavior, has unintended consequences. Executives can articulate goals like "growing faster in the future" without really contemplating how many customers that will mean winning over the competition and what it might take to get customers to change their behavior.

In "Trash the Calendar," we'll examine the world of strategic planning, which tends to happen every year at the same time whether we want it or not. Businesses all seem to have figured out that customer behavior, in their worlds, all happens to have a correlation of +1 with the earth's rotation around the sun. Our observation is that it doesn't, and businesses need to vary their planning schedules to match the time period for behavior change.

In "Defy Expertise," we'll examine the use of what we are calling "syndicated data" in organizations. Syndicated data are available to everyone for purchase from third-party sources. Businesses use these data to make critical decisions every day, often missing a critical idea – everyone has access to that data, so no real competitive advantage can be gleaned.

Examining behavioral patterns of our customers is probably the most reliable and valid way to learn about their attitudes and preferences. We'll examine why observing behavior is better than asking them in "Upend Insight."

In "Lose Control," we'll discuss the explosion of phase-gate innovation systems and how they are applied in a one-size-fits-all manner. Projects with different levels of risk and uncertainty can't leverage the same process and expect good results.

We'll also discuss in "Stomp Out Platitudes" the kinds of behaviors we need to reward (hint: It's not taking a lot of risk and failing). And in "Embrace Impermanence," we'll discuss organization models and why, we believe, that it's not a good idea to create too much permanence in any organizational structure.

Let's begin the *Detonation*.

# PART II

# BLOW UP YOUR PLAYBOOKS

CHAPTER 4

# *Dismantle Your P&L: Why Revenue Should Be the Last Thing You Worry About*

I n 1995, a then up-and-coming doughnut chain in Canada, Tim Hortons, was ripe for acquisition, and Monitor was helping a client evaluate its potential. The chain had declared publicly that its goal was to get to 2,000 stores by the year 2000. Clearly the price that anyone – our client or another bidder – would be willing to pay for Tim Hortons would be predicated on their faith in achieving this goal. Our team began investigating the assumptions underlying its sales targets.

Was 2,000 by 2000 anywhere close to an achievable goal? Canada had already, according to reports, the most doughnut stores per capita of any country in the world, and certain cities, such as St. Catherines, Ontario, and Moncton, New Brunswick, were particularly saturated – maybe as much as one doughnut shop for every 20 people. Figuring out just how many locations existed meant taking on the mind-numbing task of obtaining the yellow pages for every major city in Canada from the Toronto public library and hand-counting the doughnut chains in the listings. It took days.

The goal was to see what levels of saturation it would mean across Canada if Tim Hortons were to get to 2,000 by 2000.

We assumed that if markets added doughnut stores, and Tim Hortons kept – or grew its share modestly, then we could pressure test its growth assumptions. Naturally, our conclusion was that it was highly unlikely that Tim Hortons could make its store target and hence its revenue target in such a saturated market. We completed our financial forecast by assuming costs would continue to behave consistently with the proportion of revenue, as they had in the past, and delivered a very defensible conclusion.

It was all a moot point. Before our project was complete, Tim Hortons had sold itself to Wendy's, which could afford a higher bid because of the prospects to expand into the U.S. market. But even though it didn't matter, the team got it wrong. Way wrong.

Tim Hortons did achieve its 2,000 stores by 2000 and now has roughly 3,500 locations in Canada and more than 4,000 globally. (Steve – who had to hand-count all of those locations – is still annoyed that he can now figure this out in less than 10 seconds on the Internet versus those days in the library.) So where did we go wrong?

For starters, Tim Hortons challenged the notion that locations had to be stand-alone, freestanding locations. They started to install kiosk locations in gas stations, which turned out to be a strong growth driver as consumers loved being able to fill up their cars and themselves for a drive. They disproportionately took share from their competition by focusing on great customer service, branding that tugged at the heartstrings of Canadians, and an expanded menu that increased the relevant occasions that consumers might consider going to Tim Hortons.

We had assumed they would continue to have a space in a world that looked like it did the day before. Tim Hortons was the *cause* of the world being different. Why did we get it wrong? Because it would have been really hard for us to defend a forecast that had no basis in previously demonstrable facts.

Our Tim Hortons financial forecast is not all that different than typical financial forecasting processes in organizations today. A stylized version of a typical financial forecasting process goes something like this.

When organizations ask what they think they'll earn next year in terms of revenue, it's usually some function of looking at what they've done in the past, comparing it to "expert forecasts" of what the industry will do next year, thinking about how they'll increase their share (it's always increase, isn't it?), and then landing on a revenue goal. Once they have that revenue goal set pretty much in stone (because once it's spoken in a meeting, it's not getting changed), they ask what profit they want to make. That tends to be a function of what they've promised the capital markets or other important internal groups, or what they might need to make to fund obligations such as debt servicing and the like. And then, and only then, do they turn to costs: "knowing" their revenue, what can they afford to spend to make their profit targets?

Then the budgeting process starts in earnest. The "gap" is established between costs that organizations think are fair and necessary against the targets for revenue and profitability. Rinse, repeat, year after year after year.

And then the organization misfires in the first quarter, and it all gets thrown out the window. They have to "reforecast" and start taking costs out again. The cycle continues.

And just to check that these weren't our own observations, we asked a large sample of established businesses to report behavior in this domain. Nearly 78% of respondents reported that their companies start their forecasting with a target financial outcome.

## ANALYZE THE BEHAVIOR

Effectively, the typical financial forecast process is predicated on several faulty bits of conventional wisdom. The core assumption is that the future will be the same as the past, but it manifests itself in a number of assumptions about the world that simply don't make logical sense.

First, it assumes that companies have an inalienable right to have revenue continue in a predictable fashion into the future. The fact that most forecasts *start* with revenue effectively makes the assumption that *our customers will keep coming back if we just keep it up*. And what's the thing that we keep up? Our spending, of course. And for that, we largely presume that spending will continue to follow a predictable pattern of the percentage of revenue that it occupied in prior years. (Our research indicated 68% of companies forecast costs based on a percent of revenue target.) We recently tried to address this head-on with a client asking them to imagine what their revenue might be if three very different external worlds scenarios took place – and the revenue estimates came back within a few percentage points of each other. It's a decidedly human trait to be challenged in decoupling the future from the past.

This pattern reflects no reality that we've ever inhabited. In fact, reality literally works in the *opposite* way. Costs *create* revenue, not the other way around.[21] By not asking "why" revenue ought to behave consistent with the past, you're missing the underlying cause of your revenue – your customers' behavior. Each year, you have to give customers a reason to behave favorably toward your business. Whether it's simply to continue to buy your product or service, switch from a competitor, or agree to pay more, there has to be an underlying cause. It could be as simple as a habitual purchase (such as buying the same brand of milk every trip to the store) or a locked subscription plan, but if you're not asking why your customers behave the way they do, you're more likely to miss how that behavior drives revenue. And by thinking about what behavior needs to happen to cause revenue, you then naturally have to think about what your business needs to spend to cause that behavior. Sometimes this might look like it might have in the past. Many times, it won't. Unfortunately, businesses rarely ask the questions at this level of granularity.

Further, while businesses often gloss over the underlying behavior they need to drive to achieve revenue, they also frequently underestimate the impact of competitive moves because they aren't knowable at the time of the forecast. The implicit assumption becomes that competition will act as they did in the past, which, too, is obviously flawed. In our survey, around 75% of respondents' companies budgeted cost by starting with what they spent last year.

Revenue isn't granted by historical financial performance; it has to be earned and fought for in the marketplace year after year after year. And, over time, most marketplaces tend to become more competitive, not less, making the fight harder and harder.

The second reason is a corollary to the first. If you tend to presume that the past trend line will continue, you minimize opportunities to do more with less. Could you achieve the customer behavior you are targeting *while spending less?* By not focusing on the behavior clearly, as we need to for revenue, we miss the opportunity to ask if we are spending too much. Businesses have tried to target this phenomenon by using a technique called zero-based budgeting.

Zero-based budgeting (ZBB) forces an organization to assume that its budgets go to zero at the start of each year and that every dollar of spend needs to be justified. It's intended to address the phenomenon of anchoring budgets on last year's spend. The technique was developed by Pete Pyhrr 50 years ago when he was a controller at Texas Instruments Inc.

Pyhrr was looking for a way to shave costs when companies are going through periods of change. ZBB was applied in government under then-Georgia governor Jimmy Carter but was not widely embraced by Fortune 500 firms. More recently, ZBB was adopted by Brazilian private-equity firm 3G Capital during takeovers of giants such as Kraft Food Group, Burger King, and Heinz Co.[22]

ZBB is a good start and the principle is sound. As you'll see in the following section, you must pair this approach with a clear understanding of the desired behavior you're trying to cause with your spend.

Another unintended consequence of financial forecasting, as it's practiced today, is that it focuses management attention on understanding why the plan was different than what transpired in the real world, rather than on what actually matters: improving performance. At most companies, considerable infrastructure is dedicated to tracking and managing plans and then analyzing and explaining any negative variations. Once a plan is complete, the organization spends untold time and energy understanding why the real world is different than what is on paper – at the expense of spending that time on making the performance in the real world better. Unfortunately, positive variations rarely get the same level of scrutiny and therefore no one really knows how good performance *could* have been under different conditions.

Comparing to plan takes our eye off how we are performing for our customers *in the real world*. Every dollar we spend explaining differences relative to plan could be better spent understanding how our organization is performing, in the eyes of our customers, relative to competition. And when the focus is on meeting or beating a *financial* plan – rather than on customer behavior – it creates incentives to make decisions that may not always be best for the business in the long run (but they are good to help make plan and maximize

Me Inc.!). Comparing to plan doesn't actually tell us what the *cause* of the performance might be. So as organizations sit and show, happily, they're ahead of plan, many factors that would otherwise be bad for business, such as meaningful swings in share within customer segments regarding future profitability, can be hidden.

Finally, companies assume that actually having a rigorous financial plan will help them win in the marketplace relative to what they might have achieved without spending the time on it. We are unaware if this has ever been formally tested in a valid way, but we do see the knock-on impact of having a plan. Because we have a financial forecast, we can't help but compare success to the forecast, rather than to competition. Businesses care deeply about how well they forecast results, often more so than what they are achieving in the marketplace against competition.

We aren't the first people to point out the challenges associated with financial forecasting practices. But we'd pose two questions:

1. What's the rationale for organizations spending so much time and energy on it?

2. What do they hope to gain?

Planning processes provide a *feeling of control* even though organizations can't control all the variables that impact their business results. This is a very human tendency. Our brains react very well to feeling in control. We seek out comfortable surroundings. It's why we have long-standing habits or enjoy things that we did in our youth. Things that are known are more comfortable to us, and uncertainty, generally, causes anxiousness.[23] A great deal of scientific research has been performed on this relationship. The results tell us what intuition may have already discovered: Uncertainty diminishes our ability to efficiently and effectively prepare for the future. This leads to malfunctions in human thinking that we refer to in a general sense as anxiety. The most common feature across anxiety disorders is "aberrant and excessive anticipatory responding under conditions of threat uncertainty."[24]

We mitigate this feeling of anxiety by adopting cognitive defenses against uncertainty. Behavioral economist call this *illusion of control* bias. When subject to illusion of control bias "people feel as if they can exert more control over their environment than they actually can."[25] This illusion of control can lead to all sorts of ill-advised behavior from driving too fast on the highway to engaging in overly risky investment activities – even ignoring signs of exponential disruption as they stare directly into the face of your business.

In *The Design of Business*, Roger Martin, former co-head of Monitor and dean of the University of Toronto's Rotman School of Business, discusses the concept of reliability versus validity.[26] Reliability refers to the ability of the test, if repeated often, to generate the same outcome. Validity refers to the ability of a test to measure what it is supposed to measure. IQ tests are often used as a mechanism to explain the difference. The reason IQ tests are so popular is that they are incredibly reliable. Scores don't change much over time. Therefore, people who administer tests can point to them and not be baffled by changes to test results. But an IQ test is only valid to the extent the results correlate with success in the real world. And that link is more spurious. As it turns out, predicting real-world success is a lot harder. But people like the reliability of the IQ test and still use it year after year. There's nothing wrong with reliability. In fact, a good test needs to be both valid and reliable.

Organizations fall in love with reliability because it supports their need to feel in control. Reliability acts as a security blanket. But year-over-year need for reliability feeds a strong driver of conventional wisdom – that our "models" continue to be valid year over year. Consider the case of marketing mix models – those that try to determine the optimal allocation of marketing dollars across different media types (e.g., television, print, outdoor, digital). These models once suggested that television spending continued to offer companies the highest returns, despite observable changes that should have suggested otherwise. For instance, there were increased instances of ad-skipping leveraging DVR technology coupled with consumers spending more and more time on digital media. Both of these trends should have led marketers to shift spend to digital media faster. But marketers were slow to migrate their spend, primarily because the models that evaluated media mix really hadn't evolved to appropriately reflect the outside world. As a result, despite profound changes in consumer behavior, marketers failed to change their behavior.[27]

Simply put, the model became invalid. It was created for a world it understood. Now that world had moved on, and few organizations thought about challenging the validity of the model. The model became the decision maker rather than someone challenging the validity of the model. Financial forecasting works in the same way. When we are generally close to the results we forecast, our beliefs in the forecasting process and the way it is performed are reinforced. Knowing that it will be very hard to get reliability-seeking organizations to abandon these processes entirely, we aim to increase the validity of the processes that exist today.

## HOW TO APPLY CORE *DETONATE* PRINCIPLES

Does that mean that organizations should just forego financial planning altogether? If the choice were between planning the way most organizations do now versus doing no planning at all, it would be about a push. The amount of time and resources saved would be astounding, and if those resources were plowed back into better customer insights or things that delight the customer, the trade-off might be worth it. Having said that, we think there is a better way to plan that would give organizations much greater insight on what really matters, help them create something both valid and reliable and help them learn about their customers.

The core principle that we want to apply is to *focus on the subatomic element of business – behavior*.

Develop business plans around the customer behavior that you want to cause, and have financial plans inexorably linked. In other words, financials become – as they are in the real world – the outcome of customer behavior.

A simple way to put this in practice is to ask the question, "What broad customer behavior objective would most help me achieve the business results I want to achieve?" Broad behavior objectives for existing customers might include:

1. *Keep buying* my product or service in the same way you are buying it today *and potentially pay more for it.*

2. *Buy more* of my product or service for the same reason you are purchasing it today.

3. *Buy more* of my product or service for a different reason than you are purchasing it today.

Broad behavior objectives for prospects who aren't customers today might include:

1. *Switch* to my product or service from a competitor's product or service.

2. *Decide to purchase* the category of product/service I offer (and my business would get some share of customers entering the category).

Of course, these are very broad categories of behavior, but we find them helpful as a starting guide for businesses to clarify their objectives. And you might find that different segments of customers have different behaviors that will drive business results. But once you set a behavior objective, you then need to further specify the series of customer behaviors that will lead to the behavior objective. And you must do all this in the context of a shifting technological and competitive landscape.

Let's say you are a branded milk producer. For your existing customers, the behavior objective is to keep buying your brand of milk over others. For many consumers, their milk choice is a habit that they have developed over time by shopping at the same store, on the same day, for a long period of time. While many consumers might buy a different brand when they run out to the convenience store to purchase milk (as convenience stores rarely have the same breadth of brands as grocery stores), they return to purchasing their "regular" brand when they return to a regular, habitual grocery store trip. For milk producers, the goal ought to be to reinforce the habits that support their business. But these tactics need to take account of the broader world. What if shopping habits are disrupted by different grocery options, such as delivery services? Or worse, what if you start subscribing to a meal delivery plan, where all the ingredients you need are curated by a third party. Now, you don't even get to pick your milk brand – someone else does. In this example, the tactics are good – until they are not. If habits around your behavior objective change, you need to change your spend on how you achieve your business objective.

An effective tool to aid businesses in focusing on behavioral outcomes is having a customer journey map. This is the story of how the customer arrives at performing the behavior that is advantageous to your business. By having a clear picture of the different ways customers can arrive at the advantaged behavior, businesses can decide on tactics they can use to influence behavior (and determine how much they cost), which would have the end result of achieving revenue. In this way, businesses can ground their financials in real-world customer behavior.

To take this out of the abstract, let's imagine we're a new local restaurant in New York that wants a neighborhood family to try it for the first time. A few years back, the customer journey to decide what to eat looked pretty much like this.

The most important thing restaurants could do was to ensure they ended up in the menu drawer. So they always included menus in every bag when delivery was there, and, probably more effectively, they asked their delivery people to slide menus under the door of adjacent apartments when they delivered to another customer. This was effective and cheap advertising – end up in the menu drawer and you were in the consideration set. If you weren't, then you weren't.

Of course, journey maps evolve, and it's critical to stay current. Over time, the menu drawer became menupages.com where restaurants could publish their menus and customers now had an unlimited set of options. Here, a new behavior to cause emerges for restaurants – how to, in a world of expanded choices – cause customers to choose to order from your restaurant above others. Reviews on menupages.com and elsewhere, along with word of mouth, became even more important to drive the behavior of trying a new restaurant.

And then, seemingly overnight, menupages.com became insufficiently functional for many families, and food ordering and delivery services such as Seamless, UberEats, Caviar, Postmates, and others developed. This created the new journey map that looks like this:

- The family arrives home, tired as usual after work.

- They sit down on a couch. Someone pulls out a phone. "What do you want for dinner tonight?"

- "How about that new Thai place?" "Can I order online?" "No, you have to call."

- "Forget it, I don't feel like doing that darling." And opens up the app and starts scrolling.

So our new local Thai restaurant might have a few behaviors they could try:

- Get the family to not use an online platform, but rather call your restaurant directly and order.

- Get the family to switch to an online platform where your restaurant is located and away from one where you are not.

- Sign up for the online platform where the family already goes to regularly and hope they choose your restaurant over the others they order from usually.

- Be on the online platform the family orders from and promote your restaurant so that it shows up on the top of the list.

- Advertise generally so that the family is more likely to choose your restaurant from among others when they go to the platform of choice.

All of these behaviors – collectively or individually – could increase the likelihood that the neighborhood family tries the new restaurant. Now the work becomes what things the restaurant can do to get the family to behave in a favorable way. Those things cost money and can be reliably forecasted because they are within our control.

Once you have a set of activities for how you'd change behavior, you can develop an estimate of what each would cost to put into the world. This will help you decide which you'll choose to do on a large-scale basis versus which you might want to test. This is a far better way to estimate your costs than simply a percentage of revenue, as they are tied to specific and tangible outcomes in the real world and not artificial judgments of what "percent of revenue" is appropriate.

Finally, to tie it all together, you need to understand what the value of the behavior change would be to your organization. If the family changes their behavior in any of the manners described above, what would that lead to in revenue change for the restaurant? How much more frequently would they order? Would it change what they order? What is a reasonable expectation? Or better, what kind of change would it take to justify the cost? If the behavior change would lead to a disproportionate revenue increase relative to the cost, then you should do it. If the behavior change wouldn't drive enough revenue, then the cost probably isn't worth it. But this analysis is really only valid at the behavioral level. Once you start abstracting too far, it loses meaning.

Importantly, you can tie this together with the timing of your plan. You can monitor behavior and continually retest whether your desired impact is consistent with your hypothesis. The plan becomes more of a hypothesis test than a formal budget – one that continually gets tested.

All of this returns to the core principle of grounding your business in the subatomic element of changing behavior. Financial results are the outcome of underlying behavioral changes. If you consistently stray from the behavior that causes financial results, you implicitly assume that the behaviors that caused the past results are simply continuing in the same ratio or patterns into the future. This assumption is increasingly under pressure in a more discontinuous world. As a result, grounding financial plans in customer behavior is a way to make financial forecasts more valid – and therefore useful – in the future. If things don't go to plan, at least you'll have an immediate sense of what you need to work on with your customers.

# CHAPTER 5

# Trash the Calendar: A Strategic Planning Schedule Is Largely a Waste of Time

H ave you ever heard this in your organization? "We had such a great strategy. It was brilliant. We just couldn't get it to work for us." We hear that all the time. As we reflect over our own careers, this is probably the most common complaint we hear from companies when they undertake strategy work. They just couldn't make it work at the end. People often put this off as the difference between strategy and execution.

To figure out what the problem is, we have to go back to how the strategy was developed – and that's rooted in the planning schedule. Most organizations do something like the following. They task a bunch of (supposedly) smart people to go figure out what the company should do. Those smart people go off somewhere (usually off-site) and study a bunch of data and come back with an answer. And most of the time, everyone agrees with just how smart the strategy is and collectively decides to pursue it.

Then they turn to someone in the room, usually not one of the people who figured out the strategy, and say, "Go execute this."

And that person throws up just a little bit in his or her mouth.

Well, maybe it's not quite that bad, but it's not far from the truth. We would make the following observations about how strategic planning is broadly done:

- There is a season for planning.

- There are typically templates and/or a set process.

- Strategic planning is deeply oriented around meeting a financial objective or the outcome is a financial objective that is not usually accompanied by a logic for why the objective makes sense or under what conditions it might change.

- There is a predetermined time orientation to the plan – be it an annual plan, a three-year plan, or a five-year plan.

Let's explore each characteristic a bit further. First, we see tremendous seasonality in how businesses undertake their strategic planning. Typically, companies tend to create annual plans or longer-term plans toward the end of the year, coinciding with budgeting processes. You can almost always tell when an organization is in the midst of planning season as calendars fill and the discussion around the water cooler is about "how much is going on." And this happens each and every year without fail. Instead of planning season, we might perhaps call this decision season. In our survey, around 95% of respondents reported that their companies have a seasonal approach to planning.

From these numbers, we can see that strategic planning is typically coupled with annual budgeting. So, companies often frame strategic planning goals around a financial goal. Businesses evaluate choices – or "options" – on their ability to make the numbers.

Businesses also create arbitrary time horizons – in one-year, three-year, or five-year plans – without really considering when the best opportunity would be to revisit decisions. (Around 80% of respondents reported their companies had plans that fit this description.) In our experience, plans are rarely based on external factors made to be reevaluated when sensible based on the outside world.

Finally, there are the dreaded templates. Planning season wouldn't be planning season if it weren't for the plethora of templates. There's nothing wrong with templates per se, it's just that in many cases, they never really fit perfectly. Businesses apply them without looking for ways to tailor templates to their distinct needs.

## ANALYZE THE BEHAVIOR

Let's start with the notion that planning should be done annually. We've always found it curious that planning needs to align with the earth's rotation around the sun. We suppose that, at some point, in agrarian societies, this made some sense. Now, while there are most certainly businesses with seasonality, we're sure that, in other cases, powerful computers would allow for planning periods that deviated from this interstellar phenomenon. While we allow that sometimes planning around a calendar year might make perfect sense, it's inherently arbitrary.

For example, some industries (such as software) have a relatively fast "refresh" rate versus others (such as aircraft manufacturing) that have long lead times and capital intensiveness with orders placed well in advance.

So while annual planning isn't necessarily wrong, it's not necessarily right either. So why not make time a variable in your planning process? Even if you have shorter-term plans and longer-term plans, we don't know why each plan needs to be of the same length as its predecessor. Circumstances, not astronomy, should determine the lengths of your planning horizon.

In other words, don't treat your strategy like it's deli meat. It doesn't have a *predeterminable* expiration date. Your strategy *may* expire, but by trying to decide, in advance, how long the strategy will last is a guarantee that one of two things will happen. At the end of the expiration period, either you'll open your strategy "fridge" and smell something off and turn up your nose, or you'll waste time refreshing a strategy that might not need to be refreshed. Additionally, naming a strategy based on the year of its expiration, as we often see (e.g., our 2020 strategy or our 2025 strategy), only makes it harder for its creators to declare it obsolete. Cognitive dissonance as a result of personal embarrassment at "getting it wrong" will make it more likely that executives defend strategies that deserve a closer look.

The core *Detonate* principle to apply is looking at the subatomic element of behavior.

You should plan around behavior change, not the calendar. Here, we'll examine it in two buckets – customer behavior, as for financial planning, and employee behavior. Your planning period should reflect realistic times related to change both types of behavior in the context of the external environment.

For customer behavior, your planning period should reflect the minimum amount of time you need to test whether your actions are having the desired impact. If you're a chain of gyms targeted at women 40 years and older, and the behavior you want to drive is for women who aren't exercising regularly at any gym to join your facility because you offer an entirely different regimen, then your planning periods should be flexible enough to test several variables. You might want one longer planning period to determine whether undertaking this is viable overall, and a few shorter planning periods to refine various ways to change the behavior. If the model proves viable over time, you can continue seeking to increase your share in this segment or expand to try and serve others. All told, your planning period should reflect a realistic time frame to know how customers respond to your value proposition as declared in the plan.

You must also address employee behavior when determining your planning period, especially if you are a larger organization. We define strategy using the method described in Roger Martin and A. G. Lafley's *Playing to Win* – the Strategy Choice Cascade.[28] Martin and a number of our Monitor (now Monitor Deloitte) colleagues developed this approach. Since the book does a terrific job of describing strategy, we won't repeat it here, but the five choices when setting strategy are:

- What is your winning aspiration?
- Where will you play?
- How will you win?

- What capabilities do you need?

- What management systems do you need?

## Strategy Choice Cascade

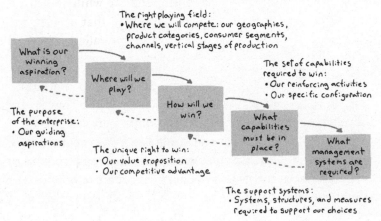

Winning strategies ensure the answers to these five questions are self-reinforcing. Your "where to play choice" is supported by your "how to win," which are in turn supported by choices your organization makes to create and enhance capabilities and manage its business.

When companies choose to pursue different where to play and how to win choices than they have in the past (such as targeting different customers with a different value proposition), they should be supported by new capabilities and management systems. This means employees inside the company need to change their behavior. That takes time, too. They need to learn new skills or the company needs to evolve to do things differently.

Like customer behavior, changing employee behavior can take considerable time (especially in the context of a broad-scale transformation), therefore companies might think about evaluating over a longer period of time the ability to actually create the capabilities and management systems for which the strategy calls. In shorter periods, they might evaluate the ability to make progress against milestones toward the development of those capabilities, all the while confirming that the organization still feels confident that it can build the capabilities and management systems called for in the strategy. The planning cycle is really never-ending; once you finish, you have to cycle back to the beginning and reevaluate your assumptions. This is another way to start testing other behaviors that can help you grow.

Your planning horizon should center on the time it will take to understand whether you can do the things necessary to change *customer* and *employee* behavior to achieve your goals in the marketplace.

## ASK, "WHAT NEEDS TO BE TRUE?"

Another simple method can help determine the right time to refresh a strategy. This tool, also discussed in more detail in *Playing to Win*, is asking the simple question, "What needs to be true?" This basically forces the person or people deciding on a strategy to articulate all the factors – both internal and external – that need to happen in order for the proposed direction to be the right one for the organization. Every time you make an important decision – such as setting a plan, you should write all the things down that need to be true for that plan to be the right one. There are a whole host of benefits – writing it down forces the organization to get clear on its logic and allows people to return and learn about their decision making if things don't go according to plan. But most importantly, this question illuminates exactly when you know it's now time to create a new plan. *It's when something that needs to be true is no longer true*. If that happens before 2020 or 2025, then you better adjust course. But if 2020 comes and goes, and all the things that make your strategy the right one are still in place, keep going!

It's that simple.

You don't need a predetermined time period populated with assumptions about the future that are invariably wrong, or at least the timing for which things are almost certainly going to be different in the real-world relative to what they were when you forecasted. But just look for signs in the world that you need to change the plan, and when they happen, revisit and/or change the plan. You might not find that the plan needs to change much, but maybe it does. This should be the core operating principles for all plans – those that are short and longer term in nature.

## LEVERAGE SCENARIOS FOR LONG TIME HORIZONS

Certain types of choices require businesses to have a point of view on their long-term potential. Whether it's significant investments (such as plants, real estate, acquisitions) or capital structure choices, we know it's sometimes important to have a long-term point of view. We have a tendency – as humans – to just assume what we know today will continue unabated into the future. This is the "dragging and dropping" syndrome that takes all the assumptions of today and extends them into the future. Dragging and dropping is not a bad thing in and by itself, but it's the underlying assumptions that businesses must increasingly check – that all your interactions with the external world, that cause in-turn, the financial performance that you achieve as a company, will still exist as you wind the clock forward. In some cases, this can be a perfectly good assumption. But if the environment surrounding your business is evolving faster than ever (which our clients say more than they have previously in our careers), this implies that simply dragging and dropping is no longer appropriate. Plans that don't address the underlying assumptions of the business really aren't all that valuable.

So, what would a better way look like? Let's start with your assumptions about the outside world. You can't predict the future, but you can predict the future won't be exactly like the past, which means you can leverage certain tools to imagine many possible futures and place your business accordingly. You'd likely see that your plan would perform very differently in those worlds versus the world of today. This is known as "scenario planning."

Scenario planning – in a generic, non-business-oriented sense – can trace its origins back to the military strategists of World War II. These commanders used war gaming as a tool to evaluate the efficiency of their potential war theater strategies against various possible enemy actions. After the war, scenario planning became even more ingrained in military strategy as the U.S. Department of Defense and the RAND Corporation (a nonprofit think tank) utilized it as a key component of their Cold War preparations.[29]

In the business world, scenario planning rose to prominence in the 1970s as a key strategic tool for Royal Dutch/Shell. Championed by Peter Schwartz, scenario planning allowed the company to consistently outperform its peers in the oil business when forecasting oil prices – a key component of any oil company's success.[30] Schwartz took his scenario expertise and founded Global Business Network (GBN) in 1988 – bringing scenario planning capabilities to both his clients and the forefront of strategy consulting.[31]

Scenario planning reveals spots where you might want to make very different decisions or build in some flexibility. For instance, say in one scenario there was regulatory relief from a burden to your business that would create a windfall, but it also might increase competitive pressures. So how might that future look? The economic underpinning to the business would drastically shift, so you probably couldn't simply drag and drop the spreadsheet.

And what would happen if some kind of technology was invented that dramatically increased the speed and accuracy of your service, using no humans whatsoever? How would that impact your business? If you're the incumbent leveraging human labor, probably not terribly well, but if you could invest and be the leader in technology, it might be great. Scenario planning highlights the places where your long-term plan relative to today's future could be meaningfully different, not just a bit up or a bit down, which is what traditional spreadsheet scenarios create.

To use scenario planning well, you might imagine how the current business, as planned, would perform in those worlds. This is different from what people usually do when creating scenarios, which is planning for "a bit up" or "a bit down" but largely in the same world. That's just trying to figure out where you are on the distribution. We suggest avoiding the urge to land precisely where you might be on a curve and instead understanding that you might be entirely on a different curve.

Coming back to the regulatory relief example, let's say a windfall came through. Would you have enough capacity to take advantage of it? How would your competitors react? Would the increased profitability invite new competition from adjacent industries? Or would the windfall largely benefit the existing incumbents? These are the questions you need to ask before you can engage in productive spreadsheet planning. And if you're not thinking about these questions, what's the value in the forecast? It becomes precise but largely inaccurate.

It's also important to imagine a world where your service can be automated. Would that cause you today to look for ways you could be the disruptor instead? Or would you ask, "If that happens, am I going to go out of business anyway?" Would the best strategy be to milk the existing business and seek tactics to delay that disruption as much as possible (e.g., by emphasizing the benefits of human interaction with your customers)? Both might be plausible, but thinking through the ways the world might be different forces those to be the core elements of your plan, not whether margins will be 48 or 49% in 2023.

Businesses must treat their planning processes as a thinking exercise, not a template exercise. While it's perhaps getting cliché to say that the pace of change is increasing, this should only increase the importance of not falling prey to conventional ways of undertaking planning. And executives need to avoid the temptations of false precision. Often undertaking the exercise yields more of the benefit than arriving at the answer does. If you already know the answer that you want, and your organization is well aligned to produce the answer you want, then you can save yourself a lot of time by declaring the answer yourself. At least you'll be able to spend the time elsewhere.

## CHAPTER 6

# *Defy Expertise: Syndicated Data Create Zero Advantage*

S teve's first meeting with a client was during his summer internship at a consulting firm in Toronto more than two decades ago. First business trip, first client meeting, first meeting with a chief executive – all wrapped up in one day.

Steve was working with a New York City–based diversified apparel company, which wanted to understand the prospects for its various lines of business during the coming three years. What did the experts think? Steve's job was to help amass a variety of perspectives and analyze which parts of the business were well positioned and which parts weren't. Day after day, Steve had been picking up the phone to call different industry publications to ask for back issues and to interview their editors.

During the flight Steve sat next to his boss, Peter, to rehearse how they'd walk through the presentation. Peter would deliver the presentation, but if he needed any backup on the sources of the data, he'd kick Steve under the table to speak.

The meeting took place in the CEO's office. The first several pages of the presentation included the update on the prospects for various components of the business – Steve's section. As Peter began to discuss page 3, the menswear slide, the CEO interrupted and said: "Are you sure? You've got the market growing at 3.1%, and I thought it was only supposed to grow at 2.5%."

The kick came under the table.

Steve quickly opened his Mac Duo Dock laptop from his Queen's University backpack and checked his source for the data. He confidently replied, "I got that from *Menswear Weekly*." And then there was a long pause. Steve squirmed under the glares of Peter and the other partner, who were clearly now worried that this summer intern had just taken them into a very bad place on the first pages of the presentation.

The chief executive then pushed the intercom button for his assistant. He said, "Jane, do we get *Menswear Weekly?*"

"I don't think so."

"Let's start ordering it, okay?"

The tension in the room dissipated, and Peter and the partner smiled. After the consultants left and were standing on the streets of New York, the partner glanced at Steve's Queen's University backpack. He turned to the 21-year-old and said, "Don't you have a briefcase?" Steve answered, "I haven't gotten around to buying one yet." The partner reached into his wallet, pulled out some cash, and said: "We've got some time before our flight. Why don't you take a walk and buy yourself one while you're in New York? You don't go to CEO meetings with backpacks."

## ANALYZE THE BEHAVIOR

In retrospect, that first client meeting was like a scene out of *Mad Men*. They just don't happen like that anymore, starting with the enormous amount of labor it took to pull together the data in a coherent and synthesized way. Back in 1995, companies that took the time to understand all the available perspectives had a real shot at having an information asymmetry advantage – knowing something their competition didn't.

Today, the weeks of Steve's work could be replicated in minutes. But companies still largely behave the way they did 20 years ago, using external information as the most important factor when making important business choices. In our survey, it was reported – not surprisingly – that around 85% of respondents' companies subscribe to published industry data reports, and more than one-half (55%) of respondents said executives in their company ask for this syndicated data before making important decisions for the organization.

Syndicated data are a typical best practice with a double-edged sword. On one hand, you can't ignore information that could have potential value in understanding the world. On the other, it is dangerous to rely on syndicated data as your only weapon against the competition. Still, we repeatedly see companies looking at syndicated data and not probing for deeper insights or seeing choice in what the data reveal.

A typical scenario happens like this:

1.  The customer data arrive and the team of analysts tells management what they say.

2.  The team slices and dices the customer data to reveal which segments of the landscape are the most profitable and the fastest growing . . . maybe the data even also reveal insight into what those profitable and fast-growing customer segments want.

3.  The company chooses to follow the data – almost blindly – and disproportionately focuses on that fast-growing and profitable segment, and figures out how to give them what they want.

Why is that so bad? It seems like a completely reasonable thing to do. Why wouldn't you want to serve the fast-growing segment? Why wouldn't you want to serve profitable customers? Why wouldn't you give customers what they want? It all seems like common sense. But when you consider the source of the insight, you should pause.

Your competition has all of these data and insights, too.

So how might this story play out? You and your competitors all figure out that this customer segment is really attractive, and you all focus your resources on doing pretty much exactly the same thing. You give the customers exactly what they say they want. And because you and all of your competitors advertise, all the customers know that they can get the same thing from all of your competition. So they now expect exactly what they want, but because all of your competition offers the same thing, customers shop around for where they can get the best price.

The fastest-growing, most profitable segment quickly becomes the most heavily competed, and profits come down. The best thing you can say about this is that the customer wins.

This may sound ridiculous, but the pattern is not all that uncommon. You see it in beer. The largest, most attractive segment in beer is the young male segment. So virtually every major beer company advertises its product as the major ingredient in "having fun," whatever the fun might be. If you show a party with lots of attractive people, usually in an outdoor space, with barbecued food, you pretty much have the majority of all beer advertisements in the U.S. It's also true of the American airline industry, where everybody copies one another on everything from ticket prices, luggage fees, and boarding processes to upgrade policies, earning status, meals, and cancellation fees. As Youngme Moon writes in her book *Different*, soon everything just gets "lost in a sea of sameness."[32]

Sure, you should stay aware of publicly available data and information. It would actually be worse to ignore it. But don't let lazy thinking creep into how you *use* the data. Knowing that your competition has the data, too, should frame how you use it.

To illustrate the point of staying aware of publicly available data, let's return to the story of the Oakland A's. At first, the A's were the only team that went "all in" on analytics to reveal where conventional wisdom had, perhaps, steered teams wrong. If you recall, the A's got rid of the sacrifice bunt. The fairytale ending from a Hollywood movie would have the A's becoming a baseball dynasty.

The truth is far from that. Because there wasn't anything proprietary in what the A's were doing, other teams quickly jumped on the bandwagon, including those that were better funded, such as the Red Sox, the Yankees, and the Cubs. It turns out that Moneyball is a good game, but Moneyball with actual money attached allows you to play even better. Perhaps a more important lesson is what happened to the teams *who didn't jump on the bandwagon* of analytics. Predictably, they fell behind.

In 2015 – more than a decade after the A's adopted the Moneyball strategy – ESPN ran a story, "The Great Analytics Rankings," in which they reviewed professional teams in a plethora of sports and ranked them based on their adoption of data-driven decision making.[33] There were major league baseball teams that ESPN ranked as "all-in" or "believers" that consistently performed in the bottom half of the league from the 2015 to 2017 seasons. Additionally, there were teams that ESPN considered skeptics that made the postseason in one or more of those years. In other words, we can't say that the adoption of Moneyball techniques is a precursor for success. However, during that same 2015–2017 time frame, teams ranked as all-in averaged 86 wins per season while teams ranked as skeptics or nonbelievers averaged only 73 wins per season. So when everyone practiced Moneyball, it wasn't enough to guarantee a winning season. But *not* adopting a Moneyball strategy when everyone else had was a good way to have a losing season.[34]

## APPLYING THE CORE *DETONATE* PRINCIPLE

The *Detonate* principle that applies here is the beginner's mind.

A beginner might say something as simple as, "We should measure what you're trying to do" – and not necessarily measure what is easily available. Yet companies frequently rely on what external data are available and drive decisions from there, rather than deciding which measures are the right ones given the objectives. Over time, the strategy becomes oriented around trying to drive improvements in the publicly available data, because that is what is managed. This does not necessarily drive business performance.

Instead of using only syndicated data and risk, falling into lazy thinking, companies should seek ways to *create* proprietary data and insights. Done properly, this allows you to make moves your competition can't see or wouldn't have made based on the data they have. (Remember, data should support decision-making. That's different than allowing data to *make* decisions.)

Three key points to remember about data are:

1.  If it isn't proprietary, then you should assume your competitors will eventually arrive at the same insight (or that they have already).

2.  Your proprietary data are only as good as the questions you ask the data to answer. So you need to ask sharper, more effective questions.

3.  The conclusions you draw from the data are valid only to the extent you believe the behaviors gleaned from the data are likely to continue into the future. As we have pointed out, the future will be different from the past, in many ways.

Are we skeptical about data? Far from it. The world of big data gives companies more opportunity than ever to get to the deeper levels of understanding about their customers and their underlying behavior. But if you don't use data creatively, even sophisticated companies can fall prey to "following the data" and missing the big picture. Classic examples of companies falling prey to their data exist (and continue to compile). Take the early adopters of customer data and analytics – primarily via digital customer loyalty programs – in the retail industry.

These pioneers exploited the competitive advantage of their proprietary data to make massive gains in market share in the mid-1990s. As one would expect, these loyalty programs and customer data collection quickly became an industry best practice. Other retailers began to emulate – and even improve on – the actions of these early adopters. Their data quickly went from proprietary to syndicated, but they continued to act as if their data were a source of competitive advantage.[35] They needed to evolve, but their behaviors became ossified best practices, and instead of repeating their past creativity and inventing new ways to have proprietary insights, they doubled down on tactics to which everyone had access.

As the advantage of the early adopters evaporated, they failed to adjust their strategic choices. Competitors that had narrowed the data and analytics gap now turned to focus on developing their own sources of competitive advantage in areas such as operational efficiency and customer experience. This led to a number of high-profile declines. The early adopters fell prey to their data and suffered the consequences.

To avoid this pitfall, you should implement mechanisms that can accurately and impartially assess their data for any proprietary value (in other words, ask the question, "Does my competition have access to this information, and if not what is the time frame until they smarten up?").

Proprietary data can really be a gold mine for making higher-quality choices faster – if they are set up quickly. But you need to gauge the status of your proprietary data regularly to understand when they have eroded for to the point of syndication – or run the risk of falling prey as so many others have.

There are several ways that companies can apply a beginner's mind to thinking about what data should drive decisions.

## Create proprietary data

This is not a simple task and entire books could be written on this topic alone. Still, if you don't create proprietary data in a data-driven world, you are likely competing from a disadvantaged position, as your competition also knows everything you do about the world.

Have proprietary data be an outcome of your business model. Customers come into a store – that's data. Visit and browse a website – that's data. Do you know who those customers are? Which customers came to a website, and who browsed what? How long did they spend? What did they buy, if anything? From where did they do this? What device? What location? What promotional material did they see in advance? All of what we've just described is easy in today's world – it's there for pretty much any company that's able to invest a modicum of resources into information design and collection. This feels like table stakes to us, but at least it's taking advantage of data only your company has. You do run the risk that your data are inferior to another company's proprietary data, but at least you'll have something that is unique – and you can figure out how to make the data better over time.

## Create a series of never-ending tests about customer behavior

To make the data better over time, you need to create a reaction among your customers with something specific. It might be an offer. It might be promotional material. It could be as simple as trying something new when they come into the store. You're running experiments on the subatomic elements of business – customer behavior to understand what their drivers, barriers, and motivators are. And importantly, every test needs to be run against a control – a group of similar customers that hasn't been exposed to whatever new thing you are testing. This way, you're more confident the test has triggered the change in response. Over time, you'll start to create a rich mosaic about the behaviors of your customers (and prospects) that can help you make more effective business decisions, faster.

## Create a series of never-ending tests about cracks in your business model

In an era of disruption, it's amazing how surprised companies are when the disruption happens. Most of the time, they weren't looking – or at least, not in the right place. For instance, Jim Keyes infamously said that Blockbuster didn't compete with Netflix just a few years before Blockbuster went bankrupt, primarily because of that competition from an alternative business model. To combat this, look for the few core, underlying behaviors that create the foundation for your company and create proprietary data that constantly tests for cracks in your own business model. This is your canary in the coal mine test. Every business could – and should – create one.

Such tests might look like the following:

- Mall traffic statistics for retail locations to answer the question, "Do people still like to go to physical stores to browse and buy?" We know many retail outlets track these statistics closely, but we wonder how many run real tests (beyond promotional) that would give customers new and different reasons to visit stores. For example, were some stores dramatically redesigned? Did it matter?

- Purchasing patterns by OEMs to answer the question, "Will downstream customers continue to buy through distributors?" Many B2B companies sell through distributors assuming that (for example) OEMs like the efficiency of buying from a consolidated source . . . and in doing so, sacrifice some of their margin to those distributors and forgo the opportunity to build deeper customer relationships. But if OEMs decide that buying direct from component suppliers is simple and easy in the digital age, that would allow for a completely different business model.

## Rinse and repeat

By repeating these steps, you can learn new ways to direct your company.

Harrah's Casinos provides a nice capstone example of a company that figured out a long time ago that data mining on customer behavior is how to create value in the casino business. In 1998, Gary Loveman left Harvard Business School to be COO at Harrah's, a middling Las Vegas casino. There, he put into action a plan to achieve the simple yet powerful philosophy that he had been teaching students in Cambridge – identifying the most profitable customers for his business to get them to shop more often. Loveman created a loyalty program called Total Rewards, replacing the then industry standard of casino managers doling out "assorted freebies – drinks, meal coupons, comped rooms – to gamblers based on guesstimates of who was betting enough to deserve them."

Loveman gave gamblers a magnetic card to insert into machines before betting to provide a data-driven picture of who his biggest customers were. By tracking actual purchases and gambling, Harrah's loyalty program was able to customize its rewards to give individual gamblers what they actually wanted. Harrah's even customized hotel rates to customers based on how much money they were likely to lose in the casinos. Under this data-driven approach, Harrah's activity and value skyrocketed – in 2005, they acquired Caesars Entertainment Inc., which, at the time, was the gaming industry's largest acquisition. As they purchased more casinos, the value of their past activity went up – they could now apply all that learning to new casinos in the empire.

If you get the discipline of producing proprietary data and habitually using it to learn, you can enter into the same cycle as Loveman's Harrah's – and create your own unique position in the industry.

By definition, your business must do something that others cannot – and that applies to your data strategies as much as it does to any other part of your business. Remember, the more you follow the "best practices" of your competitors, the less different you are for your customers.

# Chapter 7

## *Upend Insight: Customers Can't Tell You What They Believe*

T exas Hold 'Em, a variant of the card game poker, has been around since the early 1900s but exploded in popularity in the early 2000s because of exposure on TV, especially the World Series of Poker. Two cards, face down, are dealt to each player who undergo a round of betting followed by "the flop" where three "community cards" (which all the players can use to make a hand) are revealed face up in the center of the table. Another round of betting happens followed by the revelation of a fourth card (the turn), with a round of betting, and a fifth community card (the river). A final round of betting ensues. At each round of betting, a player can *check* (choose not to bet) or *bet*. If they bet, the opponents have three choices – call (match the bet), raise (up the bet), or fold.

Steve recently learned at a charity poker tournament that a truism in poker is that you can't learn anything about your opponents if you don't bet. If you play passively – that is, if you check when you have the opportunity to do so – your opponent controls the pace of the game. They could be strong (have a good hand) or they could be weak – you don't know. If you want to get information about your opponent, you need to force them to make a decision. Making someone commit to a course of action reveals considerably more information than allowing them to defer their action.

This tends to work with experienced players. They would fold if they were weak or call/raise if they were strong. They could be bluffing of course, a risk you'll have to assess as well. This is a good way to learn something about those around the table. But betting into the inexperienced players, on the other hand, is a bad strategy because the information isn't all that valuable since they tend to misvalue their hand strength. Against these less experienced players, a better strategy is to play your cards relatively straight.

At that same charity poker tournament for his daughter's preschool, Steve took an aggressive stance against his experienced finalist, raising every hand pre-flop. He eventually took home the Apple Gift Card (it's all about the kids though) and a new-found appreciation for the value of putting opponents to the test.

Why discuss poker in the context of this book? Because the most reliable way to get information about someone is to force them to make a choice and see how they respond. Had Steve taken his opponent aside, in a calmer moment, before the tournament, and asked how he would have responded to Steve's aggressive strategy, we're sure he would have said something like, "I'd just re-raise you." But in the heat of the moment, with chips on the line, people act differently.

The same can be said for how people buy things. But if we trust customers to tell us what they want, they will – invariably and unknowingly – lie to us. It's not their fault. They don't really know themselves. Yet, most businesses act as though they can. Instead, as we'll explore more fully later in this chapter, businesses should *stop asking*, and *start observing, simulating, and inferring*.

## ON CUSTOMERS AND WHETHER THEY'RE RIGHT

The basic equation of business is simple: A company creates value for its customer and – ideally – is compensated for that value at a rate higher than its cost to provide. Under this equation, the two primary drivers of the company's margin are the precision with which it can anticipate what a customer wants and the degree to which it can drive operational efficiency. For decades, companies have fine-tuned approaches to market research and cost reduction in a quest to optimize those two drivers. It's a close call on which has become a more exacting science: the domain of conjoint analyses and part-worth utility or that of Six Sigma, target costing, and design for manufacture. The world's most successful companies have created entire departments and training courses to ensure that the best practices of each are handed down to generations. While the continuing quest for operational efficiency makes sense to us, the one to better understand and analyze what customers tells us does not: It's increasingly an act of delusion.

Harry Selfridge coined the phrase "the customer is always right" more than a century ago. As proprietor of London's Selfridge's department store, he built a business around the notion that retailers should listen to their customers and provide excellent service. Unbelievably, that was actually a novel concept at a time when many businesses actively sought to mislead customers to make a sale. Echoed by other retailers and then across all sorts of businesses, the maxim stood the test of time and helped to fuel a whole industry devoted to understanding what customers think. But most organizations take the quote literally, which is a problem.

Of course, the customer isn't *always* right. Even Selfridge himself, we're sure, would have (albeit politely) told a customer who walked into the store and asked for an 80% discount. Some customers are unprofitable and should be fired by the businesses that serve them. Still, it's critical to delight your customers day in and day out, making it more likely that they return again.

When you combine a literal interpretation of Selfridge's quote with an assumption that customers can *tell you what they want*, you get into a vicious cycle that looks like this:

- Believe the customer is always right.

- Therefore, I'll just ask them what they want.

- The customers tell you what they think they want.

- Give the customers what they want.

On the surface, this *feels* conceptually right. It appeals to the rational part of our brain. But for all of you who have designed products to meet all the reported needs of customers and then seen them fail upon launch, this is the issue. In many cases, customers will tell you what they think they want – but those wants won't translate into behavior in the real world because many factors beyond what we think we want influence our actions in the real world. It's not that customers aren't well intentioned; they are. But social scientists have shown time and time again the size of the gap between expressed preferences (what customers say) and revealed preferences (what they actually do).[36]

Consider perhaps the most basic of purchases – replenishing your carton of milk, as we discussed previously. If consumers were asked all about the qualities they want in their milk, they would "overreport" their preferences for qualities such as *fresh*, *organic*, *local*, or other predictable qualities that you might name if you were trying to pit one brand of milk against another. But more often than not, the occasion determines the brand chosen. If you're running to the convenience store to pick up milk because you ran out, you are quite unlikely to go to a second store if your "preferred" brand is unavailable in that location. If you move to a new neighborhood and your local grocery store doesn't carry your old preferred brand, you're more likely to switch milk brands than drive to get the old brand. Finally, the most likely way to understand what brand of milk you will purchase on your next trip is to ask what you purchased on your last trip (as about the behavior – not about the preference).

Milk buying – for most consumers – is a habit, and the only way to effectively change behavior is to disrupt the habit in some way. Simply giving the consumer their preferred qualities in a brand of milk and putting that next to the brand they've always bought is very unlikely to yield a successful change.

Higher involvement purchases are slightly more fraught. In those situations, customers perceive the risk of getting the choice wrong to be higher and therefore obsess over the deliberation – and their motivations – more than they would in buying a tube of toothpaste. Take a story out of real life.

Geoff was in the market for a road bike recently. Having watched his wife become consumed with the sport, he figured he should probably jump on the bandwagon if he ever expected to see her on weekends again. He knew very little about the machines when he went to the shop, and soon discovered just how deep that ignorance ran. He was led through all the relevant choices that he needed to make in order to configure the right bike for himself and came to (somewhat) understand the options behind the choices. He answered myriad questions about what he wanted to achieve, what hurt when he exercised, how often he imagined himself riding, etc. When he was done and had ended up with something that he had spent more than an hour helping to design and which cost roughly 10 times what he had expected to spend, the spiraling commenced. What else could he use this money for? Would he really ride as often as he imagined? Are there better ways to get exercise and isn't this whole biking thing a bit of a fad? Plus, it's dangerous, right? And what does his wanting to "catch up" to his wife in a sport say about their relationship and his place in it?! Maybe if he wanted to get cycling exercise, he should go the Peloton route instead just so he doesn't run the risk of infringing on her private space.

Geoff walked out without buying a bike.

As it turns out, offering more choice, while it feels like you are giving the customer "what they want" can be paralyzing, as it was to Geoff. In 2000, researchers at Columbia University sought to understand the impact of selection on purchase behavior. They compared shopper behavior in two real-world situations. Under one situation, customers had a selection of 6 gourmet jams at an upscale grocery store. Under the other, there were 24 types of jams in the display. What the study revealed was that while the broader choice display made 40–60% of customers stop more frequently, purchase behavior was quite different. Only 3% of consumers purchased from the 24-jam display while 30% of consumers purchased from the 6-jam display. The incremental choice made decision-making harder, not easier, even though it's what the customer would have indicated they want.[37]

Years ago, a company such as Schwinn, with limited options, might have been able to ask customers which model they might prefer and get something back that was more reliable. Something as simple as good, better, best get consumers to respond in a more reliable way. But today, the configurations available with many bike options make it considerably harder for customers to reliably indicate preferences, especially for a newcomer like Geoff. The experience of building his bike increased his involvement to the point that he was overwhelmed with the feeling that he was making the wrong decision – and it wasn't just because of the price.

Recent research in the fields of cognitive psychology, neuroscience, and behavioral economics have challenged the long-standing ways companies have learned about customers. The world now has a much richer understanding about how people learn and make decisions.

## ANALYZE THE BEHAVIOR

That people are bad at predicting their own behavior has long been a well-studied topic in psychoanalysis. Almost 15 years ago, Timothy Wilson wrote *Strangers to Ourselves*, exploring the notion that the adaptive unconscious completely obscures any insight we might hope to have to how we will behave in certain situations.[38] This means that if you're asking consumers to explain *why* they did something, the insight is probably low, but if you're simply asking consumers to report on *what they did*, it has better reliability.

We're not here to argue that taking data from the market as a source of inspiration is a bad idea. Conversely, we believe that such a finely honed skill will be one of the most important bases of competition moving forward. We are here to argue, however, that companies should stop investing in certain types of market research. Specifically, companies should *stop* trusting insights generated from these methods:

- Quantitative surveys that broadly ask the customer to answer the question "What do you want?" Typically, these are of the variety that have "rate and rank" statements relative to the purchase of a particular product or service.

- Qualitative focus groups and group interviews.

- A miscellaneous bucket that we'll label "Sales said so." (More on this later.)

We've broadly shared in our earlier stories why we can no longer ask customers to tell us what they want. We now know that their actual behavior is tied to processes they can't explain, found deep in their unconscious. These surveys incur the double whammy of being specious on the ability to link the outcomes of the surveys to real world behavior *and* having accumulated such a slew of process and orthodoxy baggage that they are a huge source of wasted spend for most companies.

Market research manuals today have become so rigid and overloaded with instruction that researching organizations have to perform extensive work before customer data are even generated – the following instructions are a sampling from today's research manuals:

- Establish goals for your communication plan.

- Create an advisory board for research outreach.

- Develop a sampling strategy for identifying the right population to survey.

- Collect data that already exist about communities targeted for your study.

- Identify potentially similar programs or research to your own initiative.

- Format questions to measure: awareness/interest/importance/past or future likely behavior/satisfaction/preferences.

Research scientists spend weeks or months designing survey instruments that adhere to accepted guidelines around length, mix of question type, breadth of topic, and stimulus complexity. Once the data come back, statisticians spend so many weeks, months or even years using such techniques that the first two hours of any research readout are devoted to explaining the survey analysis instead of getting to the results.

There's nothing particularly bad about the first five bullets. It's the last question that really fails the test. And there's nothing wrong with spending weeks or months analyzing data that are valuable. But too often these processes are treated as rote. We should avoid asking dumb questions or following processes without thinking.

Focus groups are equally problematic. Exhausting sessions behind one-way mirrors stretch to three or four times their necessary length so that each executive see a focus group in person (because there's "no substitute for hearing directly from customers!"). That leaves the poor moderator half insane from hearing the exact same point said slightly differently 60 times in a row. Focus groups are also more subject to the impact of group dynamics and leading moderator questions. When moderators have a hypothesis in mind for what they're trying to extract, they can't help but ask questions in a particular way to generate the right answer. And the tendency of one or more members of a focus group to influence the perspectives of others is particularly challenging. The final issue: Customers don't really know why they perform particular behaviors in the first place.

But perhaps the greatest waste comes from systems of "Sales said so." This tends to be more dominant in B2B settings, when the primary source of customer information comes from sales reports and anecdotes from sales visits. Though not as formal a technique as quant surveys or focus groups, businesses give these research data even greater credence because they presume that if a real-life buyer said it and we respond to the request, we'll make a sale. Unless you set up your system to have customers reacting consistently to specific stimuli from the sales team and you measured the response across your customer base, these anecdotal conclusions are also specious. They can't be generalized to an overall pattern, and fulfilling one-off requests may lead companies to make suboptimal choices regarding their broader customer base. These categories of insights fall into the same category as when an executive says, "I showed it to my daughter and she preferred the blue one." It's just not statistically significant.

So those who create insights about customers need to wrestle with two types of situations. The first is when we are trying to understand a current behavior. Here we are in the field of the *known and knowable*. The consumer has a behavior, and we're trying to understand why they do what they do. The second is an unknown behavior because it doesn't currently exist. We have to create the behavior. This is the moral equivalent of Henry Ford's famous (although likely apocryphal) words: "If I had asked my customers what they wanted, it would have been a faster horse." You can't conclude something won't work if you don't show it to customers or ask them to buy it. *Remember, if you want to know what your opponent is holding, you have to bet!*

And the greater challenge facing insight generators is that many once-knowable behaviors are migrating to becoming unknowable. Businesses can't study them using research methods that rely on predicting customers' future actions based on past experience. Several forces will all be combining to make future scenarios in which a company is creating value for a customer increasingly difficult to imagine. First, experiences with personal technology in one domain will pervade expectations about experience in all other walks of life. Why shouldn't a procurement manager have the same insight, selection, and ease of purchase when buying a widget for their company as when buying an e-book from Amazon? Second, opportunities for *how* to create value will explode in many categories. What may previously have been limited as a solution set in the physical world could suddenly become unbound with the uptake of augmented and virtual reality. Third, whole new solution categories will arrive even more unpredictably and regularly. The surprising arrival of services like hospitality without physical infrastructure and crowdsourced delivery networks will become more and more commonplace.

So what should companies do instead? In short, they should *stop asking*, and *start observing, simulating and inferring*. And we can do that by going to our principle of focusing on behavior.

We've explored the idea of *stop asking* ad nauseam. We hope you recognize why that's the case. Does this mean that all quantitative surveys should be discarded? Well, you may have noticed we've been reporting survey results throughout our book, so either the answer is *no* or we are completely hypocritical. There's nothing wrong with asking questions and then analyzing the results, so long as you are aware of the limitations of your conclusions. Specifically, it's completely fine to ask consumers to *report their behavior*. In fact, we think this is a good way, if asked properly and specifically, to understand what customers actually did. Note: We didn't say to explain why they might have done it. You can try and draw that kind of conclusion using different techniques.

In our survey, for instance, we simply ask our respondents to report whether or not their companies do something or not. There are a lot of good ways to ask customers to report behavior. One way we like is to avoid asking about *general* behavior and instead focus on asking about the *last time they did something*. This way, they're thinking about a specific time and not trying to create an amalgam of a number of situations. Some surveys ask respondents to "think of a typical purchase situation." Well, when does that happen? What constitutes typical? Is it the most frequent? Is it the preferred? What if there is no typical situation. All these assumptions – that are likely different for each consumer. It might be fun to share the worst offenders from surveys we have been sent in the last week. When that survey comes across your desk and you are asked to comment, try to change every question that asks consumers "why" to asking consumers "what" they did. Figuring out "why" is your job as a researcher.

*Start observing and inferring* is the domain of cultural anthropology and it holds the key to how companies must interact with and understand the markets they serve if they are going to thrive in an era of constant change and "unknowable" opportunities. At its heart is the ability to get as unfiltered a view on what humans are trying to accomplish in their lives as possible and to use expert insight – or observers – to understand what is *actually* happening in any given circumstance. Anthropology developed as an outgrowth of research and interest in the classification of humans and the origin of man. To account for the variety of societies and cultures, anthropology suggested taking the total circumstances of each human group into account by "considering the whole of its history, the contacts that it had had with other groups, and the circumstances that had weighed on its development." With that, anthropologists such as Franz Boaz "encouraged seeking evidence of human behavior among people in their natural environs, and going into the field to gather facts and artifacts and record observable cultural processes."[39]

Anthropology and observing processes to generate insights entered the corporate world several decades ago. In 1979, Xerox hired Lucy Suchman, for instance, to observe everyday life with Xerox's products such as copy machine usage in the workplace. Her findings helped drive understandings regarding human-machine interaction that informed product design. Today, corporate anthropology is not uncommon – our survey indicates approximately 20% of respondents' companies use it to understand human behavior – and we expect that number to keep rising.

This is called "ethnography" and companies have myriad variations on the theme. First: an example.

A company in the life science space hired our firm years ago to advise on better understanding and serving diabetes patients. This was a time when big pharma companies were just starting to understand and accept that lifestyle management and the influence of others was equally or more important to patient outcomes as therapeutic efficacy. After the requisite quant surveys and focus groups, we finally convinced our client to allow us to take some designers with ethnography backgrounds into some patients' homes. We had all participants fill out questionnaires before our arrival at their homes about their eating habits, typical grocery lists, and other incidental information to try to make our visits as efficient as four-hour wandering conversations can be.

At one home, we had been forewarned by the questionnaire that the woman we were going to meet, a single mom, had *terrible* eating habits, and a health profile that reflected it. She reported feeling depressed about her inability to lose weight and the recent news that she was technically prediabetic. She wrote that she was stuck in a rut and had no idea how to get out of it. We arrived expecting to find a pantry jammed to the edges with junk food – potato chips, candy, soft drinks – and a fridge full of leftover fast-food meals that she had reported eating at least 10 times a week, bringing any leftovers home to snack on late night. We also had mental images of a disheveled home and dishes in the sink (stereotypes are powerful) and a person bereft of hope to get healthy.

What we found instead was a pristine home and an incredibly upbeat – if significantly overweight – interviewee. The living room was bright and well decorated. The kitchen sparkled. Her two daughters' school projects covered every available inch on the refrigerator and the tackboards in the mudroom. School pictures were proudly displayed all over the walls on the stairs to the second floor. In the fridge, apart from the usual melee of half-finished condiments and dressings, was an assortment of fresh fruit and vegetables. We were puzzled: Here was someone who showed up on paper as a dietary disaster but appeared in person to have it all together. She smiled when she spoke with us openly about her life and the way she manages it and it took a long time of circuitously exploring why she does the things she does before we started to get the full picture.

As it turns out, the woman had created a complex and sophisticated façade to prevent her daughters from understanding how depressed she was about her eating habits and inability to lose weight. She was terrified that they would think less of her or – even worse – adopt some of her habits and grow up to feel a similar depth of worthlessness. So she pretended. The junk food was hidden behind travel bags in the basement. She tucked any leftover fast food into her bedroom closet when got home so she could eat it before going to bed without alarming the girls. She used cleanliness as a signal to her children that everything was all right and whenever she felt as though she wasn't coping in the way that she needed to, she turned to her junk food stash to make herself feel better—and then worse.

This is of course a particularly complex situation where psychology is deeply effecting behavior. But this woman was trying to accomplish a specific goal: She wanted her girls to grow up to be happy and healthy despite her inability to accomplish the same for herself. None of this would have been apparent from the survey we ran (which had mainly to do with adherence to prescription regimens and frequency of doctor visits), nor the focus groups that we collectively suffered through. And in reality, much of what this woman needed in her life was not something that a pharmaceutical company would presume to be able to help with. But with the arrival of digital tools and a far greater openness to partnering with others to create ecosystems of solutions, this has changed. With far greater flexibility to serve customers in a variety of ways to achieve their jobs to be done, a much wider aperture is needed to understand them in ways that they would never be able to tell you about through traditional market research instruments.

All of these methods are – at their most basic level – giving us a leg up in bringing a beginner's mind to the question of exploring what customers are trying to achieve. Because they're not filtering data through the assumptions of research designers or statisticians, they're as close as we can get to being "inside" the motivations to the people for whom we are trying to create value. This starting place of blissful ignorance will ideally allow companies to work from first principles as they imagine how to build that value and how to take it in minimally viable increments to the market as a mechanism to test, learn, and actually drive a desired behavior when working in the unknown and unknowable domains. And there is spillover value back in the known and knowable domains, as well: You can use the exact same methods to ensure that what you offer in your core markets is on the money when you launch it. It helps cut through consideration of the combinatorial clutter of possible solutions and allows us to just give customers what we know they need without asking them. And in the process, we just might be able to recoup, redeploy or make more effective the more than $45 billion that companies spend every year – dollars that are increasingly proving ineffective.[40]

# CHAPTER 8

# Lose Control: Discard Opportunity Management Systems

L ast year, between the two of us we logged nearly a million airline miles. We also are life hackers – we try to figure out all the small steps we can take to make each day slightly better. We're constantly thinking about how to best use our travel time. Mostly, this means minimizing the minutes we're waiting at an airport, unless we can do something productive (such as write this book).

Minimizing the amount of unproductive time spent at an airport is a great way to demonstrate the concepts of risk and uncertainty.

First, we have to define the objective and the impact of being wrong. In this case, the objective is to spend the least amount of time at the airport while still making the flight. The impact of being wrong might vary situation to situation. Missing the 7 a.m. New York shuttle to Washington and "settling" for the 8 a.m. is different from taking the last flight out of New York for London to give an important speech the next day. If missing the London flight means missing the important speech, you'd prefer to have more buffer time at the airport – just in case. This buffer time describes well your degree of risk aversion for any given situation. The more buffer you require, the more risk averse you effectively are (in that situation).

Why do we need buffer time at the airport? (After all, as the saying goes, if you don't miss at least one flight per year, you're probably arriving too early at the airport.) Well, there is inherent variability in the time it takes to get to the airport. This variability helps us define the concepts of risk and uncertainty. The economist Frank Knight first popularized the differentiation between risk and uncertainty almost a century ago. We discussed this in Part I, but as a refresher, you can measure risk, but not uncertainty. In that sense, risk can be "managed" by taking steps to mitigate the impact of the variability while still meeting your objective. Uncertainty can also be managed, but usually the cost to effectively manage uncertainty is considerably higher relative to the objective.

Some uncertainties – such as if your car will arrive on time, the travel time to the airport, and the length of the security line – are relatively knowable and are low cost to mitigate. They're manageable. You just need to determine your degree of risk aversion for any given situation to determine the optimal departure time. You can mathematically quantify the degree of pain of being unproductive at an airport versus the degree of pain of missing your flight. And you can figure how much buffer to leave along the way to mitigate the risk of missing your flight based on that calculation. Based on Knight's definition, these are risks.

That said, there are still more variables. Your car could get a flat tire, or into a fender bender along the way. Your driver might get pulled over for texting. You might get stuck in grid-lock so bad that it makes you want to get out of the car and walk to the airport. Knight would classify these as *uncertainties* – factors that introduce variability, but aren't knowable easily or accurately.

We need to manage risks and uncertainties differently. When the variability is both knowable and low cost, ignoring it is silly. You still might choose to set a target arrival time earlier if your risk aversion is low, but choosing not to know is akin to ignoring the risk.

Uncertainties are different. There's not much you can do to manage against them – or the cost of doing so is high, leaving you to increase your risk aversion to manage against an unwanted alternative. Take the case of the flight from New York to London for the speech. If the only way you could mitigate the chance of a flat tire was to take a private flight that would wait for you no matter what, and that was cost prohibitive, you'd just have to leave earlier to build in a larger buffer for the unknowable and accept that you'd sit an airport longer.

## ANALYZE THE BEHAVIOR

The behavior we would like to *Detonate* is a one-size-fits-all approach to risk management.

Companies typically use an inflexible risk management system and put all projects through the same set of processes and systems whether they are on the shuttle from New York to Washington or taking the last flight to London. And for the most part, they've designed systems to manage risk as if all projects were the last flight to London, which, in many instances, means more process and risk aversion than necessary, given the situation.

This is especially true in successful companies with proven business models. When faced with a choice of "just moving" versus "collecting more data" against a choice with variable outcomes, managers regularly choose more data. We don't see a lot of instances where companies appropriately dial up or dial down risk management activities relative to the actual risk of being wrong. For instance, for a software company able to push updates to its code as needed and at virtually no cost, deep analysis likely isn't necessary every time it decides to tweak its core product. Other situations require the burden to be much higher – if the cost of a wrong decision means lives or millions of dollars lost, taking time to collect and analyze data is both valuable and necessary.

While we all say we're too busy to do our jobs effectively, very few of us are willing to take the personal risk involved in declaring "enough" on analysis and forcing a decision. So work piles up and timelines grow longer and generations of new employees learn the basics of "CYA," delaying decisions until the answer is obvious and no one can blame you for getting it wrong. You can't shut down this risk management machine, which could be the downfall of some of the most successful businesses. As opportunity shifts from the "known and knowable" space – the measurable space – to the "unknown and unknowable," risk management machines lead to self-delusion and wasted time, potentially leading to a catastrophic decision.

When we asked the business community to report behaviors, our respondents said that when faced with uncertainty their companies undertook the following response:

- Around 80% required more analysis.

- Around 40% created a prototype.

- Around 50% ran an in-market test.

According to COSO – a committee dedicated to providing thought leadership on enterprise risk management – risk management "enriches management dialogue by adding perspective to the strengths and weaknesses of a strategy as conditions change, and to how well a strategy fits with the organization's mission and vision." Risk management allows executives to feel more confident that they've examined alternative strategies and considered the input of those in their organization who will implement the strategy selected.[41]

Once strategy is set, enterprise risk management "provides an effective way for management to fulfill its role, knowing that the organization is attuned to risks that can impact strategy and is managing them well. Applying enterprise risk management helps to create trust and instill confidence in stakeholders in the current environment, which demands greater scrutiny than ever before about how risk is actively addressing and managing these risks."

In its most updated framework, COSO defines enterprise risk management across five interrelated pillars:

1. **Governance and Culture:** Establishes oversight responsibilities for enterprise risk management.

2. **Strategy and Objective-Setting:** A risk appetite is established and aligned with strategy; business objectives put strategy into practice while serving as a basis for identifying, assessing, and responding to risk.

3. **Performance:** Risks are prioritized by severity in the context of risk appetite. The organization then selects risk responses and takes a portfolio view of the amount of risk it has assumed. The results of this process are reported to key risk stakeholders.

4. **Review and Revision:** By reviewing entity performance, an organization can consider how well the enterprise risk management components are functioning over time and in light of substantial changes, and what revisions are needed.

5. **Information, Communication, and Reporting:** Enterprise risk management requires a continual process of obtaining and sharing necessary information, from both internal and external sources, which flows up, down, and across the organization.

## STAGE-GATE

This is our favorite one-size-fits-approach to risk management – to *Detonate*, that is. It perfectly embodies what happens when a system is mindlessly applied without consideration as to whether the task fits its original intent. Rooted in chemical and engineering labs of nearly 80 years ago and trademarked by Stage-Gate International and its founder, Dr. Robert G. Cooper, this aims to bring data and reason to investment decisions in the product development process.[42]

Stage-Gate's premise is straightforward and – on the surface – sensible. Instead of committing at the outset to invest heavily in developing a new product (or service, or marketing campaign, or capital project, etc.), plan to run the project through a series of linear, predictable development stages, each one punctuated by a "gate review." At this meeting, key decision makers review progress against goals and decide to continue the project if it's hitting pre-defined hurdle rates on key metrics – and kill it if not. As the project moves from early conception toward reality and launch, those metrics shift from being about size of the prize and strategic fit toward more concrete ones such as technical feasibility and anticipated financial returns. Typically, the five phases of development can be summarized as:

1. Scoping

2. Business case

3. Development

4. Testing and validation

5. Launch

What's the issue here? After all, nearly every company we know today follows this approach in making decisions.

And sure, a staged approach to commitment works well. What doesn't work are these five Stage-Gate norms that are orthodoxies in themselves, and threatening to companies in the future.

## *Front-end loading*

Businesses often celebrate Stage-Gate for its ability to clear out a clogged innovation and product development system. Companies run it against a clear schedule and calendared gate reviews, forcing progression and solving the age-old problem of innovation languishing in the development system indefinitely. But this has an unintended consequence. By presuming that Stage-Gate will do its job, companies trigger an orthodoxy: All you need for a steady stream of innovations is to feed the beast. Focus on "filling the front end" of the funnel and Stage-Gate will sort the winners from the losers. Clogging the pipeline with relatively low-quality ideas, however, leads to hours wasted on subsequent evaluation. Brainstorming can be a fine activity, but most organizations practice it poorly by failing to leveraging its unique, winning capabilities and by failing to gather deep insights on unmet customer needs.

## (Bad) Data overload

Most companies prepare for a review by scrambling madly to pull together a presentation chock full of data and analysis to help the gatekeepers make a decision. But for ideas where there is not an established market or infrastructure, data can be scarce, the scrambling intensifies under time pressure, and one of two things happen. Rather than try to characterize the risk or what behavior the project must deliver to be viable, the project team makes assumptions about the potential to hit the critical thresholds. While they may be well documented (though often, given the model's complexity, they are not), those assumptions take on an air of fact and they are not explicitly marked for testing; what was once a guess turns into accepted wisdom. Or, in other more egregious cases, we've seen teams so confident in the future of their projects, they've made up the data. Their job is simply to pass the gate reviews, with eventual launch success the ultimate litmus test of their work. So what they intended to be a risk mitigation process has actually *increased*, rather than decreased, risk.

## Regression to the core

Ironically, Stage-Gate systems are best suited to manage the opportunities for which they are least needed. Teams can be most certain about their assumptions and most able to avoid the data pitfalls mentioned above in opportunities that are closest to the reality of how they operate today – the most knowable of the knowable spaces. In those spaces, there are fewer time crunches, fewer bad assumptions and fewer attempts to bend the process to the will of the team. For bolder ideas, seemingly everything increases for the working team: risk, burden of proof, difficulty in finding data, timelines, and personal risk in advocating in the face of orthodoxy. So we see teams start to make accommodations, whittling the idea back bit by bit until it becomes much more timid – because then they can defend it. What started as an attempt to allow companies to take bold steps carefully instead turns into a system to allow them to take incremental steps with abandon.

## Process trumps purpose

While many understand the reasons why their company runs a Stage-Gate process, few love the process itself. Gate reviews lie somewhere between a commonly accepted necessary evil to the most loathed of all meetings. Sometimes, companies give younger members of the organization the power to slow down or grind to a halt multi-million dollar projects in order to drive process adherence. Project teams find themselves spending more time worrying about whether they have checked all the boxes of a particular gate versus building out the validity of the idea. A system originally designed to manage down risk and to increase economic returns has morphed into one that wastes money hand over fist.

## Worshipping the kill

Advocates often cite bold decision-making as a critical benefit of Stage-Gate. For projects that might drift indefinitely, sure. But many companies have taken this just a little too far. A colleague of ours describes Stage-Gate as a "good day at the Coliseum," with the gladiatorial project teams showing up to do battle in the gate reviews and waiting breathlessly at the end for a decision from the emperor-cum-gatekeeper. Thumbs up, and you live to fight another day. Thumbs down, and you – and your project – are fed to the lions. Many executives have earned their name in this way, ruthlessly shutting down initiatives and later being hailed for decisive action. This is another unintended consequence of filling the front end with as many ideas as possible. Instead of making interesting ideas better, the Stage-Gate system kills ideas – not just the bad ones but also the good ones that don't have the requisite data to "prove" they are good. It's another vicious cycle from a one-size-fits-all approach to idea development and evaluation.

## APPLYING THE CORE *DETONATE* PRINCIPLE

We love the fact that Cooper designed Stage-Gate to enable customer-centricity, bringing the voice of the customer into the process from the very first phase. If companies executed it well, Stage-Gate forces involvement from cross-functional teams, breaking down silos and enabling integrated decision-making. But for all the reasons listed above, even if Stage-Gate takes all the waste out of the system and optimizes the burden of proof brought to the table it still only works for problems that are knowable. When you run truly new-to-the-world challenges and opportunities – things that are unknowable unless you try them – through a process that rewards "knowability," you can easily kill great ideas.

The core principle we will apply here is – once again – bringing a beginner's mind. By asking "why" they are undertaking certain kinds of evaluation, companies can better match the work done to mitigate risk and manage uncertainty to the kind of problem they face. By following conventional wisdom, companies apply a single approach that doesn't work in many circumstances. Our goal is to create a more flexible process based on the situation.

Currently, companies must manage both risk *and* uncertainty. Eventually, we believe that uncertainty will become the norm and there will be a substantive shift away from Stage-Gate systems. But for the foreseeable future, all companies must manage opportunities by effectively identifying at the outset of an initiative (a) whether it is risky or uncertain; and (b) whether the world has ever seen the type of challenge before in the form of a "precursor."

Anything that can be called risky, since we can measure it (through such methods as scenario modeling, financial forecasting and sensitivity analysis), is, by definition, close enough to the standard business of today that it is "knowable." In risky areas, the burden of proof and level of analysis we do – and how much time we take to try to understand the risk and make a decision – should vary. There are three types of risky projects and just one uncertain one:

## Low Risk, No Brainer

This is the domain of "just go do it," perhaps because lots of solutions exist already and the opportunity for immediate economic value is high. There isn't much reason to go study this to death and at best it should be subject to a highly accelerated Stage-Gate process.

*An example: Robotic Process Automation (RPA):* RPA technology is essentially a software robot, or softbot, that has been coded to be able to do repetitive, highly logical and structured tasks. It has been around for a while, and there are extensive examples and case studies across industries, especially in banking. So, when banks examined using softbots to automate higher order processes with investment banking, the right decision seemed obvious. With growing pressure on margins, and with the success in automating structured tasks, raising demands on technology seemed like a logical next step. This is where the industry was going, and it was just a matter of time before all competitors would be doing it. Choosing not to innovate seemed like a bigger risk in this situation.

## Risky, with precursor

This is where our exposure may be high, but we're highly confident about making the move because it's been applied elsewhere before – just not in our specific situation. The argument for why the move makes sense should be reasonably straightforward. Stage-Gate may be appropriate for these initiatives but burden of proof must be held low and/or the process must be accelerated.

*An example*: *Sensor-based business models and data monetization*: United Technologies (UTC) has long been an industry leader in developing high-tech industrial parts and products. In recent years, new competitors have been coming online, and UTC knew it needed to innovate to stay ahead of the game. In one initiative, it began adding sensors to its aircraft and aerospace products, initially for predictive maintenance needs. As UTC began rolling this out, it realized the data could be valuable in many other ways and actually create a whole new source of revenue from a whole new customer: pilots. Using this data, UTC decided to build a mobile platform called OpsInsights that allows pilots to view operating information from the parts and understand better ways to fly from point A to point B. UTC had a strong hypothesis that data could be used in this way to produce business value based on evidence from many other industries. So when they tested the platform and found it to be enormously successful, they were able to open up a new business model and customer set never served before.

## Risky, without precursor

These are moves for which there is no precursor or analog that we have seen from elsewhere. We really want to do our homework when opportunities fall here, as exposure (financial or reputational) is high, and we have very little experience with the move and/or supporting data in the form of other's success stories. A classic Stage-Gate system is ideally suited for this domain.

*An example: Collaborative and/or ecosystem-driven solution development:* The city of Columbus was awarded the U.S. Department of Transportation's $40 million Smart City Challenge in June 2016. The competition involved submissions from 78 cities "to develop ideas for an integrated, first-of-its-kind smart transportation system that would use data, applications, and technology to help people and goods move more quickly, cheaply, and efficiently." The solutions were generally known (or at least had an identifiable development path) but required a complex ecosystem to deliver them. USDOT awarded the prize because, according to the White House press statement, "Columbus has a holistic vision for how technology can help all of its residents move better and access opportunity. Working with industry and philanthropic partners, the city has leveraged the Smart City Challenge to raise an additional $100 million in non-Federal resources to carry out its plan."[43]

## Uncertain

This is the domain of the "unknowable." Many Stage-Gate adherents spend lots of time running around collecting data to reduce risk, in the attempt to make it more knowable. But if the action is truly uncertain, extensive research to lower your risk is just a waste of time – the only way to generate insight is to "just go do it," similar to the "Low Risk, No Brainer" category. That being said, you need to manage this differently – because of the high degree of uncertainty, you want to make the minimum move possible to learn a bit and then move again (and not just dive in and unnecessarily expose yourself financially). Stage-Gate systems must be actively avoided in this domain.

One of our favorite examples of "just go do it" is the advent of the Palm Pilot in the early 1990s. This was a time of "spontaneous simultaneity" as Apple's Newton and various other players worked with designs and technological solutions. The one who got it right (for a time) was the one who just did it.

Jeff Hawkins, one of the founders of Palm, epitomized the activity of prototyping. In the very early days, he'd work in his garage to cut multiple pieces of balsa wood into organizer-shaped rectangles. Then he'd would load a bunch of those into his shirt pocket and carry them to meetings, sketching on each one in the moment something that occurred to him as being particularly helpful at the time. Contact entry, instant contact sharing, notes, calendar access – these all started to appear on pieces of wood and craft an overall vision for the most important functionality to be built into the Palm. And unlike computers of the era, he discovered the criticality of instant-on functionality. To steal a phrase from the design world, the device ended up being "well-behaved" from the beginning because it was founded upon how people actually interacted. The rise and fall of Palm is a much longer story. But in the early days, Jeff Hawkins demonstrated the handling of uncertainty while minimizing exposure exquisitely.

An ability to build a little, learn a little, build a little more, and so on, is vital for anyone operating in the realm of uncertainty. This process is embodied in most human-centered-design-driven approaches to innovation and is consistent with bringing the mindset of "tinkerer" to the job of developing new opportunities. It can be applied to almost any process where uncertainty is inherent, though: It will be as effective in assessing, for example, how a fundamental shift in performance metrics and incentives will be accepted in a talent system as it will in the development of a new innovation platform. But without the right direction at the outset, it can turn into endless meandering. That is where, once again, the criticality of making sure a clear desired behavioral outcome is in sight as the North Star for any uncertain initiative. In the face of uncertainty, set off in the right direction with the right behavioral insight in the first place, and then rely on multiple iterations of building and testing minimally viable steps forward to course-correct your way to a good answer.

But don't confuse uncertainty with risk. And certainly don't rely on Stage-Gate to do it all.

## CHAPTER 9

# Stomp Out Platitudes: Celebrating Failure Is an Excuse for Mediocrity

In 2000, *Forbes*, which had always celebrated for its irreverent, flamboyant style, was getting ready to launch a concept the advertising world had never seen before. It had recently purchased and mailed nearly one million :CueCat barcode scanners to its subscribers.

What's a :CueCat you ask? Well, you have to imagine yourself back in the world of 2000 – Pets.com was still "thriving" (though not for long), your friends were flocking to the world of start-ups looking for the big payday they had always dreamed of, and New Yorkers were getting primed for a Subway Series. And a now extinct company, Digital Convergence, had created a device that allowed magazine readers to scan a barcode on an ad to take them to a website for more information. It's the same concept as a banner ad on a standard webpage, except that the content comes from a magazine.

The name, :CueCat, came from the fact that the device was designed to look like a sleeping cat. Creating a mechanism for people who wanted to get more information on an advertisement wasn't a silly objective (in fact, most e-zines today with advertising hyperlinking have this feature naturally embedded).

But many critics were quick to highlight the main flaw in the design: To use the product, the reader needed to plug in the device to their computer and be connected to the Internet. In the world of 2000, this meant you had to assume magazine readers were at their desks, since WiFi was far from ubiquitous. One famous technology critic called the notion of reading a magazine at your desk "ridiculous and unnatural."

At the time, purchasing and mailing nearly a million :CueCat devices to subscribers wasn't a "bet the company" move, but it certainly wasn't insignificant. The device quickly flamed out and barcodes stopped appearing in magazine advertisements. *Forbes* had wasted a lot of money, along with the focus of the sales force driving advertisers to put barcodes in their ads. For the most part, the organization chalked the experience up to learning and moved on.

Another option would have been to send a :CueCat to a smaller portion of the subscriber base, say, in a region, or, for "selected subscribers." Or even ask subscribers to indicate if they'd like one. *Forbes* just sent to everyone. It was a "bolder" way. The swagger of the company wasn't daunted. Fair enough.

But it was an unnecessary risk. Would testing it with a small number of subscribers make the company so much slower that it would lose its position in the marketplace? Unlikely. Would :CueCat really not choose to sell their devices to their competitors? Probably not, which means that there was unlikely to be any long-lasting advantage from moving first. But because it was high profile, they had to find a way to reconcile it, so they said things such as, "You can't succeed unless you take risks."

Failing larger than necessary is not a cause for celebration. *Forbes* missed the opportunity to make a minimally viable move that would have generated the same insight it derived from sending the :CueCat to a million subscribers.

More and more these days, it seems as if we read articles where business leaders are celebrating their spectacular failures and suggesting that failure is the only path to organizational learning. We have even seen inspirational posters adorning some corporate walls touting close cousins of the idea:

Embrace Failure!

Failure Is Just the Opportunity to Begin Again!

No Idea Is a Bad Idea!

Let's please stop the madness.

## ANALYZE THE BEHAVIOR

We understand that organizations are trying to encourage risk taking in an otherwise risk-averse culture, but when your license to operate is tied to your ability to return value to your business owners, carrying around a mindset that failure is okay is irresponsible and wrong.

At almost every company that we visit, we hear the company's executives say, "No idea is a bad idea" (or something similar). We understand why this mindset has grown over time: It's similar to a placebo pill that allows individuals and organizations to take risks. Thomas Watson Sr., one of IBM's founding fathers, famously said that "the fastest way to succeed is to double your failure rate."[44]

Watson's quote embodies an important truth that going "above the line" and creating business innovations requires an element of risk taking and learning from potential (if not inevitable) mistakes. But of late, companies seem to have taken this to an extreme. The idea has been applied so sloppily and with such abandon over time that it must be held responsible for a whole lot of wasted time and some truly awful ideas introduced into what is meant to be serious consideration of business opportunity. One definition of failure is "the absence of success." Anything that encourages that kind of failure is value destroying and antithetical to the mission of every company we know of.

Over the period of a week in 2017, we came across articles about two Fortune 100 companies losing a massive amount of money, time, and effort because an "innovation" did not turn out as planned. To avoid blowing anyone's cover, suffice it to say that both are virtually universally known in business circles. The striking thing about both these articles was that they centered on the value that the company got from having failed at its attempt to create a new source of shareholder value. Some of that can be chalked up to the usual saving of face that any senior executive will need to engage in when interviewed about a well-intentioned move gone awry. But these went one step further toward being celebratory in tone, enthusing about the level of customer insight that they were able to tap into on account of having launched new product or business models that ended up being damp squibs.

Reading these brought to mind the often cringeworthy conversations we have with people who are new on their journey of building an innovation capability within established companies. Usually, they have read all the right books and gone to all the right conferences and have returned spooled up and ready to repeat the mantras of the inspirational posters mentioned earlier. And most of them summarize these points with the justification that they hold true at places such as Tesla, Airbnb, and Uber: "We have to act like a start-up." The problem is, many of the companies that these people work for are the furthest possible thing from a start-up.

Start-ups and entrepreneurs have a different set of incentives than larger, established organizations. While any given entrepreneur may have various equity classes breathing down his or her neck to create the world's next unicorn, most investors in start-ups recognize that the hit rate is really very low. They expect most start-ups not to make it because only with a high rate of failure do returns from the rare successes pay for the entire system. This expectation can create incentives for a behavior in early-stage companies to work outlandish hours in order to fail fast or to overweight reliance on creativity from a lone genius to solve for a singular business model. The few start-ups that make it, not surprisingly, eventually stop acting like one. They start acting like they need to drive predictable profit and growth. They start thinking about diversifying their business model to continually evolve without destroying proven value in their core business. And, at an individual basis, they (thankfully, for most) stop working themselves to the bone. Simply, it's a different life with different rules.

To add insult to injury, those who are the most prominent evangelists of the Church of Failure end up just sounding dumb when others come to their senses and realize that in fact there are bad ideas that run the risk of destroying real shareholder value. An absence of success actually can hurt when there is real economic or reputational exposure: Stock prices take a hit and boards tighten the screws on management to improve short-term performance.

Of course, none of the failure evangelists would claim that the objective of innovation is to fail. They would claim that you could only make nonincremental innovation moves if you work in an atmosphere where risk taking is encouraged and where you don't have to worry about losing your job if your hypotheses are proven wrong.

A better system could be built entirely on the concept of Minimally Viable Moves (MVM). Our belief is that organizations in the future will increasingly succeed or fail based on their ability to learn. But you can't learn if you aren't clear about what your hypotheses about cause and effect in the world (i.e., if we make this move, we will cause this outcome). In addition, you won't learn if you don't test your hypotheses in ways that don't consistently bet the company. And you need to make sure that the organization complies with this mode, so you need to punish those who don't behave consistently with the direction. Therefore, the key components of our playbook would be:

- Demand transparency and open logic from your organization.

- Conduct never-ending experiments.

- "Punish" failing to comply.

## Demand transparency and open logic from your organization

A system of transparency and open logic – one where we all get concrete and explicit about what assumptions we are making behind the actions we take – is far better than one where a cloak of accepting failure hides bad assumptions. What do we mean by transparency and open logic? It's when the organization demands, assesses, and rewards the logic behind all decisions rather than simply the result itself.

Why is this better? Today, organizations have two broad failure modes. Either they don't challenge long-held orthodoxies and simply assume that the operating constraints, nature of opportunity, and other "realities" of the past are going to govern the future. In this mode, the very act of raising and challenging an orthodoxy will in many companies represent a real personal risk. Or they "celebrate failure" when poorly defined projects that took more risk than necessary inevitably fail.

Transparency and open logic focus the attention of the management team on the underpinning logic of an innovation or an investment so that it is apparent and testable – and rewards if the logic was right versus whether the outcome was positive or negative. One example of being a logic-driven organization observable in the world today comes from the domain of investment management. Most business reward systems are predicated on celebrating the right outcomes with – at best – marginal input on how the outcome was achieved. In a linear world where there is a reasonably clear line of sight between decision taken and impact, understanding the logic behind the decision isn't critical.

But the pace of technological advancement is making it harder to assume we are in a linear world. We are in a world characterized by rapid changes in the external environment – positive or negative – and we're all going to need to operate in one governed by a level of uncertainty that investment managers – given how many external factors they need to take into account for any trade – have been living with for a while. These managers are typically evaluated not based solely on their results but on the timing of their decisions, micro-level analysis of trades, and so on. If you achieve a good outcome with a successful trade but your logic for how you got there is faulty, you get docked. And if your logic is great but externalities prevent success, then while perhaps not celebrated, you will not be punished for failing to achieve your hypothesized outcome.

The dynamic at play here is one of openness: If you are able to make your logic clear and open to challenge at every step along the way then the collective system should be able to prevent failure by catching flawed logic.

Additionally, as you move forward into testing your logic in the real world (through – as we'll discuss – a never-ending series of experiments), then by writing down your logic, and testing it, you learn if it was strong or flawed. By simply throwing ideas out into the world without an articulated logic, you don't learn.

## Create a never-ending series of experiments

We've talked about the idea of reiterating earlier in the book. It's fundamental to how we have to think about strategy today. Doing this effectively requires a mindset of "get it out beats get it right." Instead of conversations dominated by time lines, milestones, and deliverables, they should be focused on questions such as "Can we do it faster?" Instead of hours spent trying to determine whether the right process is being adhered to in the right way, minutes should be spent asking, "Has someone else done this before and can we borrow or build upon their work?" And instead of empty statements about failure being all right and everyone left feeling just a little bit embarrassed when they hear their leaders repeating that mantra, a growing sense of pride in agility and better outcomes can lead to a virtuous cycle of success.

When you are clear on your logic, you find a way to continue to understand, using a minimally viable move, whether the logic is sound, and when you know it's sound, if it can scale into something larger. For instance, if we were trying to reverse engineer how a company such as Uber might have thought about experiments and logic, it might have progressed something like the following:

- I have a hypothesis that hailing rides from your phone and creating a community of drivers using their own vehicle can be a superior customer experience to the existing taxi market. Therefore, I want to test if that logic is correct, so I want to do a small test, say, in San Francisco, to see if people will use the service and understand what the economics are. *Test conducted and passed, therefore. . .*

- Now that I know consumers will indeed get into cars with strangers and all signs show it is a positive experience, I also need to understand whether this concept will work in other cities besides San Francisco. So I'll expand and test a number of other cities. I'm specifically testing for the ability to expand. *Test conducted and passed, therefore. . .*

- Now that I'm pretty sure the concept will work in major cities in the U.S., I'll want to run similar tests in cities around the world. *Test conducted, some passed, some did not. But failure was always small relative to the size of the company.*

- Now that I've got a successful ride-hailing business, can I launch a ride-sharing business to capture more of the market. So we'll launch such a service in selected cities. *Test conducted and passed, therefore. . .*

- Now that I'd got a successful ride hailing and sharing business, can I use my capabilities to deliver other things? Can I use automated cars? Can I deliver people to the Hamptons via helicopter from Manhattan?

Nothing really beats real-world tests for the ability to predict success in the real world. Yes, some things can be analyzed well, but in a world that is moving and changing quickly, increasingly the past doesn't predict the future. So the only way to know, is to move.

In this world, all activities presume a "market" – either internal or external – for a move. The salesperson serves the external customer directly. The human resource manager serves the internal talent base. The CEO serves her board members as representatives of the company's shareholders. Following the precepts of an earlier chapter, if we are living by the first principle of focusing all activity on driving a certain behavioral outcome, then every targeted audience for a move has an associated targeted behavior – which itself is the measurable outcome that we can use as the North Star for guiding ourselves out of the uncertain woods.

## Punish failing to comply

And in this world, failure will still exist, manifesting as a waste of resources. Specifically, it will occur when someone builds too much into the experimental MVM (wasting money), doesn't move fast enough to get to market fast (wasting time), or doesn't take the time to understand the driver of a necessary course correction (wasting an opportunity to learn). But in this world, big, unthinking failures will ideally not be tolerated except in very small doses and very occasionally. If we have created an ability to operate effectively with a system in which failure has been designed away, then it should in fact be punished when it occurs.

Said differently, in this world, we are not at all punishing people for having incorrect hypotheses. We are punishing them for failing to have them and being clear about it. We are not punishing people for trying an idea in the real world and having it not work, we are punishing them for overexpanding before their hypothesis was well proved at a smaller scale. In other words, when we punish someone, it's for the purpose of correcting their behavior to not fall prey to the lazy thinking that creates the need to "celebrate failure."

## AN EXPANDING TOOL SET TO MAKE MINIMALLY VIABLE MOVES

The good news is that increasingly – even exponentially – we will have tools at our disposal to monitor behavioral outcomes and to speed up the cycle time for course correction. New technologies such as sensors and instant social feedback can be combined with analytics to drive toward almost instantaneous knowledge of whether a MVM is a good one.

A number of companies are already taking advantage of the expanding digital tool kit, using sensors and analytics to monitor and drive behavioral outcomes. Disney, for example, is deploying sensor technology to provide immediate and actionable customer data that allows it to make fast-cycle changes to its Disney World experience. Disney's Magic Band is given to guests prior to visiting Disney World. The band, which contains a long-range radio as well as sensors, lets guests swipe onto rides and pay for food and merchandise while allowing Disney to pinpoint their location. The band couples with the Disney World app – so when guests enter information regarding their favorite rides or preorder meals from a specific restaurant, the Magic Band provides a neatly packaged itinerary for rides based on a guest's location and initiates a food order from a restaurant before the guest even sits down – waiters even greet guests by name as they enter.[45]

The Magic Band provides value from a customer experience and operational perspective. Guests are given the perception that Disney World knows what they want before they do, which creates a seamless experience more likely to yield higher spending and return rates. Additionally, Disney uses the technology to optimize usage of its employees – the system replaces employees' time spent with payments and tickets for moments of personal interactions with visitors.

Amazon similarly uses analytics to drive desired outcomes from both its consumers and vendors. Ninety percent of the company's customers use the Buy Box – the large box on a product detail page where customers can begin the purchasing process by adding items to their shopping carts. When a customer makes a purchase from Amazon, a number of potential vendors often provide that same product for sale behind the scenes. In those situations, Amazon uses an algorithm to track different vendors' metrics on product pricing and availability, fulfillment history, and customer service and awards the Buy Box purchase to the vendor who will provide shoppers the best customer experience. This ensures that customers are happy shopping from Amazon while also driving strong performance from vendors wanting a sale. This is all opaque to the customer (and often to the vendors as well), but it allows Amazon to constantly improve the customer experience, one minimally viable move at a time.[46]

Of course, not every move will need to stay in minimally viable format indefinitely. Much like a new innovation takes shape until it is a viable solution to launch in the market, at some point, we will become sufficiently confident in a move that we can use it to operate at scale. Also, like with new innovations, metrics of success will need to shift over time to follow the development of the move. In the early stages of an its development, the purpose – and the corollary metrics of success – should largely be subjective and qualitative in nature: Are we deepening our understanding of target audience needs? Does our hypothesized value proposition meet those needs?

Are we challenging the orthodoxies of our company and industry about how we create value? Only after the team is confident in the stability of the MVM should it flip to purpose and measures that are more objective and quantitative in nature: Are early adoption rates sufficient to justify continue spend on the move? Do we appear to be creating enough value to justify the expense of the move? Are we seeing others drawn to our solution in a way that we can start to see an ecosystem of value creation taking hold? And if the answer to any of these is "no," then there should be latitude to continue to test and refine until the answer is "yes."

If you are a scaled company with shareholders to answer to, failure is not an option. In the face of uncertainty, reduce forward progress to minimally essential steps of learning and adjusting. With the eradication of the nonsense about failure being a good thing replaced by a sensible discussion of how to create economic value, we just might be able to get scaled enterprises with legacy business models to perform (a bit) like start-ups after all.

## CHAPTER 10

---

# *Embrace Impermanence: Org Charts and Career Paths Are Past Their Sell-By Date*

---

S ome companies are well known for their incredible generosity to their employees. It often happens in the background without fanfare, but it is an important part of creating a familial culture and a low turnover rate. At one company that we worked with, for example, one employee was helping a friend adopt a child in Kazakhstan; the organization made sure that she had a satellite phone in case of an emergency.

The company was also very generous with 401(k) matching, so people stuck around for a long time. Take "Bev" (a pseudonym). We're not exactly sure when she started, but in the early 2000s, she had been in her job for several decades, managing billing. Because of the vagaries of building laws for private organizations, somehow Bev got away with smoking in her office. On the basis of the degree of yellow on the ceiling, Bev must have been in her office for at least 20 years. The stench of cigarette smoke was overwhelming. Papers were spread everywhere, and an old-fashioned calculator with a paper roll occupied part of the desk.

Bev was pleasant, but there was no question of who was in charge. Bev was. She spoke with a heavy smoker's voice. She had a process she had been running for a long time, and nobody was going to get in the way to do things differently. People used to joke about how they'd get around to changing the billing and layout function once Bev retired.

The business world is filled with Bevs. Maybe not exactly like her, but people don't like to change when they're settled. They've got that really comfortable spot on the couch, and they're going to sit there. Plus, when someone with a different shape comes into that spot, it just doesn't feel quite right. So they sink lower.

You can see the effect of an army of Bev on entire industries. Take, for instance, the world of advertising and media. Consumers began using more digital media by the year 2000, surfing the Internet regularly and spending an increasing proportion of their daily life wired. When companies introduced smartphones as a category, they accelerated the shift from traditional to nontraditional media as people could consume content on the go and not just on their laptop or desktop computers.

By 2017, it felt weird to call digital media nontraditional because, to an entire generation, it's the default preference for communicating. The growth was staggering and obvious to anyone with eyes and ears. Consumption of digital media usage nearly tripled from 2010 to 2015 to represent 46% of total hours consumed by media.[47]

During this period of time, we also witnessed the invention of a number of technologies that allowed consumers to skip television ads more effectively. This was not new technology. The VCR first hit the scene in the 1970s, and while few people could work the clock function to get it to stop flashing 12:00, some did use it for its purpose – recording shows and watching them at another time. But with the arrival of the digital video recorder (DVR) and over-the-top (OTT) services, consumers could now record or find their favorite shows and easily skip over advertisements or avoid them entirely.

So, naturally, given these two trends, a growth in digital media and decay in the effectiveness of traditional TV spend (why pay for skipped ads?), you'd expect to see a dramatic shift downward in the proportion of spend dedicated to TV and a rise in digital advertising spend. It should be logical, right? You'd want your brand to show up where people are spending time.

But to say the adoption by large advertisers has been slow would be an understatement. Spend on digital media did grow as a proportion of overall spend – but still represented a very small portion of overall spend. In 1999, digital was less than 1% of spend for the top 100 advertisers, growing to 8.1% in 2011, large growth for sure in relative terms, but still well behind the proportion of time spent. And most of this came at the expense of obvious targets – the traditional print industry. Television, however, basically hadn't moved. In fact, from 1999 to 2011, it *rose* as a percentage of total spend – from 62.9% to 63.1%.

In fairness, there are some things that bolster TV. It's still one of the few places where audiences can be aggregated in large quantities, so it can be inherently efficient. That being said, only a handful of shows and events fit this description. But there was another mechanism lurking deep under the surface.

It was someone's job to buy TV ads.

Yes, most large marketing organizations had appointed someone to work with traditional advertising and media-buying agencies. Typically, this was a relatively senior and central person because most advertising, historically, would have gone through that person. So it's not surprising that, even as trends against TV continued to mount, the people in this role were not exactly open to trying something different.

And when, eventually, companies gave people similar roles to purchase and coordinate digital advertising, initially they were the fringe specialists. More often than not, digital people started as part of a center of excellence (COE) available as resources to the rest of the organization when needed. Of course, being stuck in a COE is a great way for a skill to go underleveraged in a broader organization.

## ANALYZE THE BEHAVIOR

This general pattern of organizational silos dictating work that gets done is not new, nor is it a secret. And many executives use organization redesign as the first arrow out of the quiver when they come into a new role. This works for a while, until that organization structure gets ossified and companies create new silos. So it's almost a guarantee that if we:

- Have strategy organizations, we will have "important annual strategic plans that everyone must do."

- Have finance organizations, we will have "important budget processes that everyone must go through."

- Have human resource organizations, we will have "important employee survey reviews that everyone must complete."

And these are just the examples from support organizations. You experience the opposite from parts of the organization that "own a P&L." Leaders will say "I own this P&L, and since I'm accountable, I need to therefore own every single decision that hits 'my P&L.'" Of course, this works only in the smallest and simplest organizations that have a single level of accountability. In any organization with multiple P&Ls (for instance, across regional lines or across different businesses) and a matrix with support functions, someone, somewhere, is going to have to make a decision that you didn't get to approve.

This need for control and building the importance of your particular organizational silo is completely consistent with the logic that surrounds "Me Inc." – it serves me personally to augment the importance of my organization because that is more likely to augment my sense of self-worth, make me feel good and important within the context of the organization. And I naturally become defensive when people challenge whether what I'm doing is relevant.

The problem here is the presumption of permanence in organizations. If we create a role, we presume it will exist forever. Because the people in those roles benefit in some way from being in it, their natural inclination is to protect such roles. We may need a massively invasive restructuring to take groups of people out of roles that don't make sense anymore, which has the potential to be helpful but also creates new silos over time.

The *Detonate* principle that applies here is the beginner's mind.

There's a better way. Organizations must embrace impermanence in how they design their organizations and undertake work. As with many degenerative diseases, the trick is to prevent ossification from setting in initially, so we recommend focusing on prevention rather than on a cure. Here are several ways to embrace impermanence.

## Periodically shake up your organization

This could mean move people around in leadership roles, create new roles, or undertake a wholesale restructure. We've seen this practice work successfully at creating connective tissue among the people in large organizations. With frequent organizational shake-ups, no silo ever takes hold, so the underlying problem in the marketplace easily rises to the surface. If leadership understands that its internal roles are not necessarily perpetually guaranteed, then it might be more likely to act to drive collective results, versus improving its prominence within the organization.

This is decent first step, though a disruptive one.

## Engage in more project-oriented work serving internal and groups of end customers

Because customer behavior is the most basic subatomic element of business, all your work should be oriented toward that end.

Consider the internal customers, too, those who make it possible for organizations to support their end customers. Think about organizing work around customers: Whose needs do you serve? What do you need to do to serve them? What skills are required to serve those needs? What do you need to delight customers and have them choose your offer over the competition? What teams can you create to support needs? The link to the end customer must be clear. The requirements work backward, and the goals of all the teams should be synchronized with customers' changing needs.

## Resist career paths

Employees challenge companies by insisting on knowing "where they will be in 5 to 10 years." When Steve counsels people within Deloitte, he constantly reminds them that every plan he had over his career never came to fruition. Not one. Everything he thought he was going to be doing took an unexpected turn at some point, and taking advantage of serendipity was crucial. We hear these stories a lot from our colleagues and clients. Plans are usually left unrealized. Doing great and impactful work leads to opportunities with broader scope and more responsibility. But companies still publish the 10-year plan for new employees.

Today, career paths are at best a false sense of security. Reorient your people around the concept that "great work is rewarded" with more responsibility. "And we don't know precisely what you'll be doing in 5 to 10 years, but if we're successful in delighting our customers, and you are successful in delighting your organizational customers, you'll have ample opportunity to be doing really cool stuff down the road. We could try and tell you what that is, but we'd rather not make stuff up and have to explain why we were wrong at a later date."

## Diversify skill bases

Teams with a lack of cognitive diversity are far more susceptible to groupthink and conventional wisdom than teams with people who think differently. But most organizations are stocked with MBAs in important entry-level management positions, all of whom learned the same core skills because, for the most part, the core curricula at MBA programs have been the same for several decades. By taking a group of people who are all assumed to think relatively similarly and putting them on the same teams, in one part of the organization, we create the preconditions for conventional wisdom to kick in and creativity to be stifled.

You can take two actions here. First, staff teams with different types of thinkers, including designers and ethnographers. Why? Most organizations tend to ossify toward the reliability end of the spectrum – to deliver what was asked. Designers by their nature are trained to figure out how to best meet the objective and are more validity oriented, even if the solutions aren't tried and true. Ethnographers can bring the power of observation to teams and see needs in customers that others simply don't have the training to see. This applies equally to internal customers and to end customers.

It's also increasingly important to leverage the world of data scientists to complement ethnography. If ethnographers learn about customers from watching their behavior, data scientists can help teams learn about customers by creatively examining the data surrounding their behavior. Data scientists can also help a team design valid tests in the outside world that can help show how the company is or isn't winning with customers.

All of these people can work together – MBAs, designers, data scientists, engineers. Our typical approach is to put these groups into organizations with people who all think alike, but the magic happens when you put them together. As long as the preconditions for team successes hold, then we'll get a lot more creativity from a diverse group.

## Limit the size and scope of your internal organization

No organization is best at everything. Therefore, there is a limit to what you can ask of your organization without it becoming increasingly unwieldy with size.

Although not all large organizations are cumbersome, the degree of difficulty tends to be harder in coordinating a large group than a small group. Large organizations, by definition, have more people, and the more people you have, the greater diversity in a "Me Inc." you need to handle, and that becomes problematic. You're also less able to create interesting and customized approaches to meeting needs, because the larger you become, the more time and attention this takes.

Think carefully about not letting yourself get too large. Undertake only those actions that are central to delighting your end customers. Assign adjacent actions to someone else outside the organization. This will allow your business to run efficiently and enable you to focus your precious team time on the things that matter.

We're amazed that more support organizations aren't fully outsourced, given they are rarely critical to the mission. Now, because we can all work remotely, transfer data, and share things in nanoseconds, outsourcing is increasingly easy. So companies should be disciplined when they add people – is there is more mission-critical work or simply more work? If the former, great: Go out and get the best people in the world. If the latter, why not find a firm that does that for a living and have them do it?

■ ■ ■

Your organizational design should never be the cause of your actions. It should reflect what work you need to do at any given point in time to win with your customers. And because that's changing faster than ever, you shouldn't put something in place that you wouldn't be willing to blow up in a nanosecond if it was the right thing to do from a customer perspective.

# PART III

# BUILD SOMETHING BETTER

# CHAPTER 11

# *Where to Start: Pick Your Site to Apply the* Detonate *Mindset*

In 2006, a snowstorm leveled Boston. New England had already had a pretty tough winter, with significant amounts of snow accumulating each week. The driveway to Geoff's home was short enough that he used to pride himself on being able to shovel it on his own, without help from a machine, and his sons were young enough at the time to be useless beyond the comic relief they provided. As the winter ground on, the snowbanks on either side of the driveway grew to the point that Geoff needed to throw new-fallen snow two feet above his head to get it on the pile. And then the monster storm hit. It snowed for two days straight; schools closed and authorities advised against travel. In the midst of the storm, there was no reason to go out shoveling as more would just keep coming. Geoff and his sons devised a plan.

It would be the mother of all snow forts. They designed an entryway to be just outside the side door, where there was a covered porch. That allowed the door to open onto direct access to a pile of what was now close to four feet of snow. They drew a tunnel system, taking into account the swing set, and winding around to the massive snow piles on either side of the driveway. They took advantage of a stone wall that would allow for a second story of sorts if they could get some of the leftover plywood in the garage in there for stabilization. As they drew the design on paper, they became increasingly excited. In the front of the house, they drew a top-entry access point where they could drop into the fort from one of the boys' bedroom windows on the second floor. And the coup de grâce was one offshoot tunnel that went right up to the kitchen window from which they could supply the fort with hot chocolate and something slightly stronger for the adults. This fort would last until spring! They'd bring everyone from the neighborhood! After a morning's worth of design and a table full of drawings, they truly had something magnificent.

Then they did nothing. They looked over the sheets and sheets of paper and imagined with delight what it could be. But they had designed something so beautifully complex and all encompassing that the undertaking just felt too daunting. The idea of sinking the first shovel into the snow and setting off on a job that would consume the rest of the day and likely more days to come took the wind out of their sails pretty quickly. So they lit a fire and watched a movie as the snow fell around them. Eventually someone gathered the plans from the kitchen table so they could have a meal, and they moved on.

Who knows what might have happened had they just started digging at the beginning of the day instead of spending all their time planning? They might have ended up with something truly incredible. Or they may have ended up with something not much more than a snow igloo. But they would have ended up with something more than they did in trying to design the whole system at the outset.

The point of this story: Ignore the systemic effect. Instead, focus on a minimally viable move to get going, trusting that something good will come of it even though you may not have the end game in mind. The questions are what, where and with whom.

## BECOMING CHICKEN LITTLE

So yes, we need to start blowing up some of our most sacred playbooks – but we don't need to challenge orthodoxy from corporate rooftops, declaring to all who will listen that the company is in dire danger. Such Chicken Little behavior, even when warranted, rarely gets the attention it deserves and often just breeds resentment that someone is disturbing the peace.

Still, it's become a habit that businesses have to overstate threats, which has given rise to the equally powerful habit of taking such warnings with a grain of salt. Especially in a litigious world, caution signs are more about protecting from lawsuit than about preventing harm. Take the simple example of product packaging. A recent study showed that consumer-warning labels today are ineffective; they do not play a substantial role in helping consumers make an informed decision – because they're ignored.

As *Harvard Business Review* reports: "The problem with our present warning system is that it shouts 'Danger!' for both wolves and puppies. Such a system is of little value; people quickly learn to ignore warnings since they encounter vastly more puppies than wolves. The result is that when a wolf is truly present, people pay little heed."[48] If you are warning against something as substantial as the inner wirings of the corporation and its sacred playbooks, large swathes of the organization will dismiss you as a puppy – or worse.

Often, companies openly attack challengers of orthodoxy. We know these attackers generally have good intentions, high integrity, and a desire to optimize for the collective good (even as they try to advance their own careers). But when a threat to the organization's health becomes apparent, some group sets out to neutralize the threat, either formally or informally. Innovation can trigger corporate "antibodies" – those who are resistant to change and look to shut down progress. We believe that most antibodies are, in fact, good, generally acting rationally and in the best interest of the company's shareholders, especially in highly successful organizations.

In biology, antibodies are an effective and necessary part of our immune system; they bind to toxic bacteria and viruses in order to tag these invading cells for destruction – in a normal world. But antibodies also can be harmful. Unlike most infections, the dengue virus appears to be able to hijack antibodies and use them to unleash an even more severe reaction. At first the dengue infection is typically mild – not even requiring hospitalization in many cases. Antibodies can often successfully neutralize the virus. In the case of "antibody-dependent enhancement," though, a second dengue infection can use the antibodies from the first infection to enter the host cells more easily. The result is hemorrhaging, organ failure, and even death.[49]

Blockbuster has now become the poster child of a company that ignored all signs that it faced such an existential threat – and comments from its executives help illustrate just how far some are willing to go to ignore reality. In 1990, just five years after Blockbuster's founding, the video-rental business was a giant, with more than 1,300 locations. In 1993, *USA Today* quoted Greg Fairbanks, Blockbuster's CFO, saying, "Every day, there's another story about fiber-optic technology, 500 channels, video on demand." He recognized that those developments might someday allow viewers to choose from hundreds of movies that would be delivered to TVs over cable or phone lines at any time, perhaps eliminating the need for a trip to the video store. "But those stories just complicate our story," Fairbanks continued. Similarly, at the 1993 annual meeting "founder and subsequent CEO Wayne Huizenga scoffed at suggestions that new pay-per-view and video-on-demand systems [then] in development [would] sound the death knell for the home video industry." Seven years later, CEO John Antico laughed Netflix founder Reed Hastings out of the room when he offered to form a partnership between the two organizations.[50]

We all know how that movie ended.

Exponential change and the vicious cycle that we described in Chapter 2 could lead to a similar dynamic elsewhere. Antibodies will have confidence that the protective techniques that worked in the past will continue to do so. In the face of someone challenging deep orthodoxy, those same protectors will likely hunker down – using either passive or active resistance – and wait for the attacker to be neutralized. And in doing so, they will allow change to get dragged out, and the vicious cycle experiences "antibody-dependent enhancement." It's not lost on either of us that this very book is likely going to trigger antibody reaction (and may even be doing so in small or large part is some of our readers' minds). The comfortable thing to do would be to rationalize away the need to take *Detonate* principles seriously or – more aggressively – look for holes in the logic and missing definitive proof points instead of early warning signs that we might actually be on to something.

So, the question is how to use the natural good intention of these people to accelerate rather than to block progress. It would be simplistic to say that you need to start at the top. Most of the time, senior executives' support is critical to the success of any corporate initiative. At some point, that support will be valuable, but it's not the right place to start. There's just too personal and organizational perceived risk for most senior executives to defy orthodoxy. Even in the face of apparent existential threat, it is difficult to look beyond the immediacy of a successful business model and a demanding and short-term-focused shareholder base. And that only gets exacerbated if the executive's retirement is in sight.

## Where: Focus on the Core

One option is to start on the periphery of the business. Our colleagues at Deloitte's Center for the Edge have developed what we consider to be the definitive answer on how to scale edge businesses. As they see it, to thrive in an exponential world, "companies must move from innovating at a product or service level to innovating across their entire institutions. Unfortunately, traditional large-scale change efforts that challenge the core of the business often fail. Change management is not rational – it is intensely political. The Scaling Edges methodology helps businesses focus on low investment, high-growth-potential opportunities – 'edges' – with fundamentally different business practices that can ultimately transform the core of the organization."[51]

Edges are different from traditional growth or change initiatives because they align with what an organization sees as long-term disruptive shifts in the market. In the short-term, Edges are platforms for high growth that have the potential to grow the pie and scale. But in the long-term, Edges have the potential to transform the core and be a catalyst for change. The Scaling Edge theory is based on the idea that too often, change agents think that big changes require big investments. Similar to Geoff's grand snow fort, they develop an exhaustive multiyear plan, lay out a large investment pathway, and hope for a return down the line – and therefore expose themselves to attack by the antibodies and likely shutdown before they ever get going. So instead, in a fast-moving world, our CFE colleagues would encourage change agents to focus on the periphery rather than the core.

It would perhaps seem logical, then, that if you're going to blow up a bunch of stuff, you should similarly try to find an edge to try it out first. But there is a key difference here: Whereas the development of an Edge business is intended to be a semicovert operation to create something that will eventually overtake the core, *Detonate* is all about directly shifting the core from the inside; we don't think you can blow up playbooks effectively and permanently from the periphery. We think of it along the lines of an insurgency. Although we'll resist the temptation to dive into geopolitical analogies, if you want to bring about substantial change as quickly as possible with as little "blood" spilled as possible, avoid the frontal attack. Rather, start small and unnoticed, hidden from both the "antibodies" and the powers that be. Focus on a limited set of fundamental principles that – as demonstrated via small successes – gradually attract more adherents. The successes should grow in size and impact to the point that they do become noticeable to others, but the good that they are doing is so incontrovertible that it becomes irrational to attack the revolutionaries. Indeed, this clearly positive impact will appeal to the inherent desire of the antibodies to do good, and will attract them into the revolutionary fold. Eventually, there will be enough momentum behind the movement to make it unstoppable.

You have to start an insidious revolution in the core business. Only demonstrated success and progress in the very heart of what previously made a company successful will lead the well-intentioned antibodies to come aboard.

## WHAT: START WITH BEHAVIOR

Of all the principles we discussed in Part II, a focus on human behavior is the most foundational and weaves through all the rest. It also provides insight not just into what to focus on in the change effort, but also *how to effect change* – because it is human behavior within the organization that must change, after all.

The business world has long known about behavioralism and behavioral economics. As Gallup has reported, "companies that apply the principles of behavioral economics outperform their peers by 85 percent in sales growth and more than 25 percent in gross margin."[52] And examples abound of companies that – whether intentionally or not – applied behavioral economics in the course of driving growth and change.

Amazon Prime is perhaps one of the best known: A suite of features, from one-click ordering to guaranteed delivery and free media, radically reduced barriers to action and led to impressive results. At the time of this writing, the proportion of first-year Prime members who spend over $800 annually on Amazon is double those who are not subscribed; for those who have been subscribed for 4+ years, that proportion increases to a whopping 4x![53] Procter & Gamble's Febreze product suite course-corrected a product in danger of being discontinued, encouraging habit formation through behavioral modeling. The team made Febreze a part of existing cleaning habits rather than trying to get consumers to create new habits.[54] The revamped product doubled sales in its first two months, earned $230 million profit in a year and earned more than $1 billion a year in spinoff product categories. And the "Save More Tomorrow (SMarT)" program, based on concepts developed by Professors Shlomo Benartzi and Richard Thaler, explicitly uses Behavioral Economics concepts such as defaults, loss aversion, and opt-out to help people with long-term planning. In its first implementation, the SMarT program boosted average savings rates from 3.5 to 13.6% (more than 350%) in 40 months.[55]

Neither of us proclaims to be an expert in the field of behavioral economics, but we have seen enough of its practical application and impact to have hopped on the bandwagon with some of our design colleagues to tout its benefits. The starting place for how to apply the notion of focusing on human behavior goes back to our stance that it's the most basic atomic unit of business. All business is intended to drive some sort of behavioral outcome to create economic returns, and all business is an accumulation of human behaviors. Whether we're talking about driving a different outcome in our end markets, with our immediate customers, or in our own company, the logic path to pick the behaviors to focus on is reasonably straightforward:

- What are we trying to achieve as a business?

- What options for behavioral change – by whom – are required to achieve that goal and what is relative economic value of each?

- What behavioral tendencies get in the way of achieving that goal?

- What combinations of strategies can overcome those tendencies?

- How can we quickly demonstrate that a strategy or solution works?

Hot in the world of digital design these days are customer journey maps (which we discussed in Chapter 4) – depictions of all the interactions that a customer segment has with our company from the very earliest "pre-consideration" stage to the postpurchase assessment and "exit" stage. These are nothing new; marketing strategists have been creating buying process maps for decades. And indeed, when the world was just a little simpler and any actor could more readily explain why they behave the way they do, companies used traditional market research methods to populate process maps in identifying where best to intervene for impact. We believe that behavioral maps of any audience can be an incredibly valuable way to visually depict the economic system of any business and to help identify which behaviors to target. But to be helpful in a world that is changing at the rate we have described before, the depth of insight into behavior drivers and the nuanced science behind "behavioral tendencies" has to be much more powerful than ever before.

Deloitte's innovation practice – Doblin – is one of the original innovation firms to apply design approaches to solving business challenges. It's been one of the key sources of new insight in the field. Its research grew from the recognition that we can be irrational, missing the information we need to make informed choices, and often make mistakes because of processing "errors" in our brains. This all results in predictable – and seemingly irrational – behaviors. Doblin's research suggests that for any sort of behavior, there are common factors that impact the outcome, many of which lie below the surface of what the actors can explain themselves. Those factors are:

- Kinship and Self
- Expectations, Influences
- Framing
- Time Distortion

- Barriers and Enablers
- Experience

Doblin further breaks those factors down into 30 different tactics that can be used to influence behavior.

Without getting into all the detail, we've found that one of the most practical applications of this body of research comes in understanding the most common barriers to action that humans face in anything we do. There are seven:

1. Navigating Choice
2. Overcoming Paralysis
3. Navigating Impulsive Decisions
4. Grounding Abstract Consequences
5. Trying Something New
6. Overcoming Distrust
7. Instilling Self-Control

Take, for example, the barrier of Trying Something New. We see this all the time, whether it's a customer considering changing a favorite brand or an employee throwing out a revered playbook in favor of a new way of doing things. Although the people in question may not be able to express – with full honesty – why they're is unwilling to try something new, it usually comes down to one of four reasons:

1. Fear of feeling dumb by making the wrong choice
2. Skepticism of the value of the new thing
3. Lack of motivation
4. Resistance to new action

To pick just one of these to further deconstruct: The fear of feeling dumb is a common barrier to action of many types, and likewise there are a common set of successful approaches to de-risking action. Generically, we can do this by making it feel safe (e.g., by providing guarantees or indicating the "right way to act") or by providing encouragement (e.g., by providing timely and relevant feedback or by letting them practice or try out things first).

The purpose here is not to go into Behavioral Design in depth, but rather to illustrate that this is a rich field of unfolding understanding that itself will develop exponentially along with cognitive neuroscience. In other words: We have the growing insight; we might as well put it to use. Given its heritage, the reader would forgive us for being so enamored of Doblin's approach to Behavioral Design. Truth be told, dozens of similar models and tools are available and the general point is *just pick one and start to apply it.* The most direct way to catalyze the *Detonate* journey is to start thinking about, talking about, planning around and taking action on human behavior in everything you do as an organization.

## WITH WHOM: IT DEPENDS

While we can be fairly definitive about "what" to do, who you choose to start with is a bit trickier. We face this key dilemma: The locus of initial change must be sufficiently "of the core" that it acts as a revolution from the inside, but it can't be so intertwined with activities that deliver this quarter's performance that it risks destroying the company. This would defy the definition of a "controlled detonation." So if you're a manufacturer relying on Six-Sigma quality at a certain plant running at full capacity to meet a top customer's growing demand, don't slow things down to conduct ethnography on your plant operators. If you're an electronics company on the verge of launching a blockbuster next-generation product and you have trained your customers to expect a certain level of price premium over last year's model, don't start pricing dynamically based on how long a customer takes to fill out the online order form.

In all likelihood, the *easiest* place to start will be a business or functional area with declining performance and a reason to do something differently. It needs to be an area that will feel like a relevant analog to the rest of the organization as a demonstration area – that is, something other than a unicorn. And ideally, it will be somewhere with some natural-born and vocal leaders. The moment these two things come together in the ideal away is often at the point of leadership change: when those natural leaders have been moved from another part of the business to help turn around the struggler. And *who* they are matters enormously. The most important characteristic is someone who is willing to embrace change and is curious. Someone who has strongly held beliefs about how things are is unlikely to defy orthodoxy. This person might be young or old, a digital native or immigrant, but as long as they are willing to learn, they can be effective.

Of course, the *best* place to start is the business that is not in need of detonation. The one that is strong and seems to have a durable business model. Here, an act of detonation sends the signal to the rest of the organization that leadership is serious about adopting new ways of thinking to create future value.

There's a loose hierarchy of difficulty in the moves we described in Part II, and we'd recommend starting with the easier moves. In keeping with the startup mantra of "start small and scale," you must be able to book some early wins to be able to create any momentum at all. Start by looking beyond syndicated data and surveys for new sources of inspiration as you create a plan around behavioral change using nontraditional insight. After that, use fast prototyping and test-and-learn development cycles to prove that the organization doesn't need to rely on Stage-Gate. With that in hand, you and everyone else at the company should be able to stop with the platitudes about being open to failure because you've been able to demonstrate that you don't need to fail to succeed. From there, tackle the broader corporate institutions of strategic planning and P&L development on a path to eventually giving everyone confidence that organizational charts and career paths are not the way to motivate people to want to succeed.

As we've talked about this vision for the future company with some of our clients, the glee that comes from imagining such a world feeds upon itself. What if we get rid of slides as a primary communication vehicle?! What if we could implement the idea that "standing meetings" means that no meeting can be so long that it's uncomfortable to stand for it instead of sit? What if email went away?

These are grand visions indeed – and ones we would do well to dream a little about and then pack away quickly. If we start with such grand plans then we may just end there as well: putting our feet up and ignoring the sketches on the table because it all seems so daunting. Instead, we need to start with a simple, small step forward in the dark and ask this: What is the minimally viable move – the smallest possible believable demonstration of success – that we can take to prove that focusing on human behavior can lead to a positive economic outcome?

# CHAPTER 12

## *Implications for Leadership: Accelerate by Asking Better Questions*

I f this book were a conference speech, the host would invariably ask a question such as, "What one thing can this group of people go back to their office tomorrow and change and have a huge impact?" Generally, we hate this question. It trivializes the challenges of widespread organizational change and is the moral equivalent of governing by sound bite. It's just not that easy.

That being said, you can do something immediately, Monday morning back in the office: Change your questions. We all ask them every day of our teams. And every time we ask something, they go and do work, consistent with their interpretation of our questions. One of our colleagues, Jonathan Goodman, the Global Managing Partner of Monitor Deloitte, is fond of saying, "The most powerful tool executives have to drive change is their questions."[56] Yes, questions are a very powerful tool, indeed. Change the question, change the outcome.

The two of us were working with a well-known consumer products company that had a leading position in a global category and was looking to fend off competition by extending its position with innovation focused away from the product. With a little bit of coaching, the innovation team had created three really interesting concepts that had the potential to make an upcoming launch even stronger without touching the product. Yet in our interim review, the head of the division, naturally excited about seeing some things in the product she liked, asked a number of questions. As we debriefed, team members received the impression that the nonproduct component of the concept didn't matter, and they were ready to discard a lot of good work.

We took the division head aside and asked if this was her intention, and she said, not at all, she was just excited. We told her that at the next meeting, "Don't ask any product questions, even if you have them. Ask only questions about the components of the offer that were not associated with the product." Sure enough, she did just that, the team was energized again, and the offers hit the markets successfully. The point is that executive questions have the ability to immediately change behavior, intentionally or not.

This story also illustrates how much of an impact the particular presentation of questions has on your organization's behavior. Having watched executive behavior over our careers, and having experienced the challenge of leadership within our own firm, we understand that questions aren't always framed perfectly. Miscommunications happen from thinking out loud in meetings, or overly hasty responses to emails. These are real challenges. We'll admit, we've both made the mistake of sending teams in the wrong direction because of imprecise, poorly worded, or just otherwise bad communication.

## Questions We Hate

Here are the questions we find most egregious and how you can ask them better or ask different questions altogether.

## What's the ROI on this investment?

Seeking to understand the financial benefit of an investment is a fine objective, but it's one of the most challenging questions executives tend to ask. When people hear this question, their immediate stance becomes one of *defending* the investment rather than *considering* it, and they feel in the hot seat of making it their problem, rather than the organization's problem. So instead of feeling as if they are getting to a better answer, team members feel their backs are against a wall. Hear this question enough, and you'll learn to come in armed with all the facts and data you can imagine to prove your position.

Now, bludgeoned with facts and data, the executives are overwhelmed with PowerPoint slides and can't make heads or tails of the rationale for the idea in the first place. We've created a vicious cycle of questions creating defensiveness and colossal waste while rarely getting to the actual conditions that drive results in the real world.

This question is worded poorly for other reasons, too. First, it implies that you can predict market results precisely, without risk. In some cases – say, you are launching a product with a clear track record in a new geographic market without distinct characteristics from past markets – you might create reasonable estimates might be created. But increasingly, we find there are fewer and fewer such circumstances.

A better way to capture the imprecision of forecasts and inherent volatility of possible outcomes is to ask, "What's a reasonable range of outcomes of our investment?" This is a better question as it explicitly acknowledges the fact that you can't know the precise outcome and gives the space for the responder to share detail that drives the investment.

This question also forces the discussion away from the choice at hand. Yes, the organization is trying to assess whether it should make the investment, but it's actually having a conversation about absolute outcomes, not whether the investment meets the threshold. As a result, many "no-brainers" are subject to overanalysis, and organizations move slower than they otherwise could. More productive questions address both *absolute* and *outcomes* by focusing questions on whether minimum investment thresholds are met and the critical customer behavior or cost assumptions under which an investment would meet the threshold. For example, a better question would be, "How many customers need to sign up for us to achieve our cost of capital?" Another might be, "Under what combination of cost and customer assumptions do we meet our investment hurdle?" Here, the question drives at the nature of the bet the organization is making on what it can do in the marketplace, rather than a single quantitative measure.

Finally – and the top reason we hate this question – it implies that if we don't make this investment, the world will just continue as it is into the future unabated. You make many investments to prevent decline in your core business. Therefore, measuring on "incremental" against an inappropriate baseline makes no sense.

Imagine a ridiculously stylized example: Automakers today have to assess to what degree they invest in self-driving car. While there is some uncertainty regarding *when* self-driving cars will become the vast majority of cars on the road, there's not much uncertainty regarding *if* that will happen. By measuring the investment against a baseline that assumes the core business continues to grow and thrive, automakers are missing the core concept. Businesses naturally over time have their competitiveness erode without investment (because competitors catch up and create new products). It's wrong to assume you can grow for free, unabated into the future. Yet, this implies that this investment creates *unique* value over and above what we are doing today. A better way to frame the question might be, "How can we assess all the ways this investment could add value, including bolstering the core business?"

## Has anyone else in our industry done this before?

This question kills innovation, but we see it all the time. In many situations, it's about assessing risk – not about risk that exists the marketplace, but the personal risk that decision makers face. It's about preserving "Me Inc." This question is really asking, "Am I going to look crazy for doing this?" or "How hard is this going to be to get through the organization?" Those are legitimate concerns that the organization can address through company dynamics and culture, not through asking this question, which creates unnecessary and wasteful work. It usually leads to something to the effect of "let's have an offline conversation," the kiss of death in any meeting.

Let's say you're truly trying to understand the degree to which this concept is new to the industry. It's likely you know (or at least should know) whether the competition is "doing this" already. So instead of asking an opaque question about *if* the competition is doing it, try asking, "*What are the advantages and disadvantages of being first in our industry?*" This acknowledges that there could be value creation from moving first, but there also can be a downside by not having the best design if you can learn from the mistakes of others. It also leads to a more productive discussion versus shutting down a conversation.

Perhaps an even better way to ask the question is, "Has this type of problem been solved anywhere else in the world?" You can create value in your industry by taking something that has been meaningfully proved elsewhere and figuring out a way to apply it to your problem. This can unlock creativity in your organization and give risk-averse team members confidence that they are not frontier explorers if that makes them uncomfortable. For example, what learning can companies creating stain removal detergent take from other places where precision targeting is important – such as the military (with increasingly precise artillery fire) or oncology (chemotherapy that kills cancer cells without impacting regular cells)?

Finally, you might really be asking, "How will I convince skeptical, risk-averse, senior management that I'm (personally) not crazy?" Instead, you could ask, "How can we demonstrate to other team members the value of this idea?" or "What analogies can we use about this idea that would help people understand its value?" A good example is when ZocDoc, an online medical care scheduling service, arrived as a successful start-up in the medical space. If you talked about disrupting medical practice management software, it might sound risky. But if you said, "It's OpenTable for doctor appointments," people would light up.

By the way, if the answer is that someone in the industry is already doing it, you likely have a different problem to discuss!

## How can we prove this will work?

One of our colleagues, Larry Keeley, coauthor of *The Ten Types of Innovation*, is fond of saying, "If you use the words 'prove' and 'it' in the same sentence, you're killing innovation." Why? Because the only way you can *definitively* prove something will work is to do it in the marketplace. And therefore, if you want something innovative, defined as something that doesn't yet exist, there is no place to prove it *but* in the marketplace. When you ask this question, your team invariably scrambles to create the illusion of proof, so you end up with mountains of slides filled with analysis, none of which really offer definitive proof. Since the work is inherently futile, the experience will suggest that innovation is hard to predict, and you will be asking for even more proof.[57]

Don't ask for proof. In fact, if you're a senior executive, eliminate this word from your lexicon. There's no such thing as proof in business, especially in a highly uncertain world. For those of you who are now thinking, "Hey, I know I'm not getting proof, but I'm not really asking for that, I just want more information," know that your teams aren't hearing that. Given their desire not to be embarrassed in front of their boss, they hear "proof," and they come back to you trying to be "bulletproof."

If you're looking for more information, simply ask, "How could we learn more about this?" This clarifies that you, too, are in exploratory mode, and it puts you as part of that journey. You're not throwing responsibility on team members to figure everything out (even though they do the work). You also acknowledge uncertainty and are placing the value on the information that informs the decision, not the decision just yet.

If you're assessing your discomfort with the current risk-reward balance, then ask, "How could we make a smaller move, quickly?" Instead of having the team cycle back for more analysis, you're promoting action, but addressing the risk-reward balance by looking for an even smaller minimum viable move. Pushing the team to test something in the world, somehow directly with consumers, and doing it faster, helps avoid analysis paralysis.

## QUESTIONS WE LOVE

Here are some additional questions that were suggested by our network. (We'd love to hear the questions you love online using the hashtag #detonatethebook.)

### What might be another possible way to tackle this problem?

We love this question because it has multiple benefits. Importantly, it doesn't immediately reject the initial solution a team might be proposing – or even one that's been done for years. That might still be a good idea. But by forcing team members or the organization to consider how they might solve a problem another way, it also forces them to come back to clarify what problem they are trying to solve. This is critical for tackling conventional wisdom because so many organization processes exist to give managers a sense of control when they increasingly *can't* be in control. Also, having a clear problem triggers a clear solution. When you can't even remember what you're trying to solve, you need to go back to the drawing board. If you can come up with multiple ways to solve the problem, you know you've got clarity. We also appreciate this question because it forces divergent thinking.

## Which customers will love this? which customers will hate this?

We like any question that forces people to think about customer needs. Many organizations fall prey to being internally focused, and questions that cause them to ask questions about why something will resolve a customer need is good. For that reason, we didn't put "Why will customers love this?" into our "stop asking" bucket. That being said, we like the formation better when you are more precise and ask about "which" customers.

That's because no group of customers is the same as another. There are always pockets of customers who have very different needs, attitudes, and, you guessed it, behaviors. Getting precise about which group of customers will love an idea is really important. If you can identify a group that loves something, you have a better sense of where you'll win in the marketplace and can better assess the economic potential of any opportunity.

Why *hate* this? Well, if you're really trying to make some group of customers love something, you'll likely cause another group of customers to dislike it. But that's good! It means you're making a real trade-off and trying hard to win with a specific group of customers. Think of some of the most loved brands in the world – almost all of them have a group of customers that would never go near them. If you're not making some group of customers hate the choices you've made, it's likely you're not trying hard enough to make some other group of customers love you.

## What behavior are we trying to change?

By now you'll know why we love this question. It focuses the attention on a clear place where we are the cause and the behavior is the effect. Whether it's the behavior of a prospective customer or a line employee, it's always critical to know what's the purpose of your actions, and most of the time, it is someone's behavior.

## How might we move faster? if we had to try something today, what would we try?

We love this question because it helps teams cut to the chase and gets teams focused on what they really need to understand. It separates the need-to-have from the nice-to-have, and it brings into focus what a minimally viable move might look like. Finally, we love this question because often teams look at what they can do for today and say, "Hey, that's not bad, we should just do it."

And smart, focused action is what we are looking to drive.

# CHAPTER 13

## Minimally Viable Thoughts

T hroughout the course of writing this book, we've ended up with the mental equivalent of a bunch of crumpled up pieces of paper in the waste bin. But rather than take out the trash to neaten up our work space now that the immediate job is done, we'd like to smooth out a few of those papers and put them out there for comment. We welcome all your thoughts, especially those that take the ideas to a new level and, even more importantly, introduce new ideas to the mix as the business world continues to change. We've created several places where we hope to make the material from the book open to building and evolving. On various social media, we'll use the hashtag #detonatethebook, and if demand merits, we'll launch a more permanent way to continue the conversation.

So let's start with three interconnected, not-quite-ready-for-prime-time thoughts.

## MAYBE LONG-TERM SURVIVAL ISN'T ALL THAT IMPORTANT

Nearly every client that we've spent any significant time with has been pursuing a strategy to grow meaningfully. Most companies act like not growing is dying. Whether driving more topline sales by entering new regions or categories, or taking cost out in times of sectoral decline, there has to be an upward trend in *some* line for a business to consider itself a success – indeed, many of the cartoons in this book are based on that fundamental notion.

A lot of the time, growth is good: If managed for profitability, it can be a source of cash for reinvestment and continued thriving. But growth is just one means to what should be the intended end: to create economic value. The key question is, economic value for whom? In a world of permanence (or at least long-term survival), it's easy to say that the economic value has to accrue to the company's shareholders and that one way to do that is to create value for customers as well. And in a world of triple-bottom-line optimization, if we can do those things while also driving social and environmental impact, then everyone goes home happy. Growth becomes the objective function.

Topline growth, in and of itself, doesn't create intrinsic value for a business. For one thing, it's rarely free. Growth requires investment in new capabilities to serve the needs of the new customers you are trying to serve. In many circumstances, the cost of finding these new capabilities will outweigh the opportunity they might create. If the growth isn't profitable in the long run because the cost of achieving that growth is too high, then it doesn't create value for the owners of the business. And companies make lots of spurious arguments about growth creating scale and platforms that can be leveraged elsewhere. But far too often we have seen companies make that assumption and then never check back to test the value against the underlying economics of the business.

The point is that growth isn't an imperative, it's a choice. And it becomes an even more uncertain choice if you release the assumption that the economic value has to accrue to today's shareholders. What if instead of trying to figure out ways to optimize pay to the owners of today, we paid attention to the gross economic value creation across all players in the ecosystem: owners, employees, customers, suppliers, competitors, and so forth. Of course, that would require some complicated moves to determine how to make sure that a "fair share" of that optimized value creation ended up in owners' hands . . . but it just might lead to consideration of a far greater array of options at any given point in time.

Just like in the U.S. medical industry, where the system spends a disproportionate amount of money on keeping patients alive just a little longer, you can destroy a lot of value by approaching growth (i.e., extended life) as an imperative, not a choice. If you choose growth, what's your legitimate alternative? In a word: death.[58]

For existing organizations, this would mean resisting the urge – when topline growth in any given category starts to trail off – to diversify into new areas. Instead, focus on driving more value from your existing business, consistently figuring out how you can take cost out of the business to deliver more profit from the same group of customers. But cost cutting is, by definition, a temporary move. If you're down that path and a magic new source of topline growth doesn't appear, then you need to be ready to unwind the business when it gets too challenging to continue to extract value. Given all the natural barriers to making this choice, we know it's an unpopular suggestion. And for a couple of guys who have spent a good portion of their careers extolling the virtues of innovation, this may sound downright disingenuous. But maybe there's something to simply driving more value from your existing business. What we can't figure out – and why this particular idea ended up crumpled on the floor – is how to know in the moment whether to innovate or unwind. We would love to hear your thoughts.

A concept we like better – especially for new businesses that don't have a legacy asset base to worry about keeping productive – is to always be thinking along the lines of a "pop-up company," extending the mindset and notion of a temporary store to a corporate scale. You can create a new business to take advantage of a clear current in the market, but dissolve it when that need dissolves. While it's not a company, per se, the Dash button by Amazon is a good example of a pop-up company. Buttons around the home, connected to your WiFi, are a good way to simplify reordering products – much easier than going to a website or even a smartphone. But as other possibilities with even less friction emerge – auto-fulfillment or ordering through a voice-activated product such as the Echo – consumers' need for buttons will likely drop. Sure, some consumers will still prefer a button, but the space for that particular product will decline over time as other options arise.

Imagine if businesses were created with that mindset from the start. They could invest all their resources in creating something special for the customer, avoiding the imperative to find adjacencies for the business and add lots of administrative costs. Instead, they could channel all their energy into serving the customers' need and – in theory – unlocking the maximum amount of economic value in doing so. And then, as the market opportunity faded, the business would just gradually unwind. If you believe that the current pace of technological advancement will continue or increase, then you can see how the half-life of relevance for any given customer offer will decline at a corresponding rate. Therefore, many companies will be faced with a fundamental strategy choice: Do you invest to keep up with technology, or accept that your offer will become less relevant over time and cut losses at the appropriate point?

## IF LONG-TERM SURVIVAL'S NOT THE POINT, THEN ARE CURRENT VALUATION METHODS DEFUNCT?

Business school students all over the world learn multiple ways of valuing a company, but the most standard is the discounted cash flow valuation. This method, simplistically, forecasts the free cash flow of the business for a certain number of years to a "steady state" (say, 5 to 10 years), and then creates a "terminal value" – the value of the business at the end of the forecast period. The cash flows and terminal value are discounted back to present day using the firm's weighted average cost of capital, which is determined by evaluating the company's cost of debt, cost of equity, tax rate, relative risk against the market, and capital structure.

In most cases, a large proportion of the company's value is in the terminal value. So what is this terminal value? In most cases, students learn to presume the business lasts forever and calculate the terminal value using a perpetual cash flow formula (FCF/WACC-g). For what it's worth, most other valuation methods are also essentially derivatives of a perpetuity calculation, whether it's the dividend growth model or "multiple" valuations that effectively lump risk and future growth into one factor to be applied to earnings, sales, or some other financial or operating measure.

The underlying premise in all these methods is an assumption that the business lasts forever. That's the very idea of perpetuity. But, increasingly this is simply a poor assumption. The turnover in the S&P 500 has been steadily increasing, and while the past is not a predictor of the future, it should be obvious to any observer that businesses, as much as they try, don't last forever.

Valuation purists would say that the possibility of a company ceasing to exist in the future is embedded in the cost of capital assumption – specifically, the risk premium investors apply to the stock. Theoretically, we would concede that point. But the risk premium in valuation is a function of the volatility of the stock relative to the market, versus an inherent assessment of the risk that the company will or won't exist in the future. Might it be better to make an explicit assumption on the probability of existence in some future years? We think so.

Just because a popular intrinsic valuation tool is perhaps flawed, it doesn't necessarily mean the capital markets are systematically overvalued. The market always clears at the price that a marginal investor is willing to pay for a stock – a behavioral measure, not an analytic one. So just because we might point out that valuation methods are flawed, the market might effectively say, "Prices are right, but we just have to adjust other assumptions to make up for it." But it makes us wonder whether we might be missing something.

## WHAT WILL BE THE LOGIC FOR BEING A PUBLIC COMPANY IN THE FUTURE?

The very notions of company impermanence and defunct valuation methods would suggest that the notion of a public company could be on a pretty shaky foundation. But even more basically, as we think of many of the barriers that cause companies to miss the full range of options they have at their disposal at any given time, they are most pronounced for the public company. Increasingly short holding periods by investors; management incentives that reward short-term performance and/or that have binary targets or dates; reporting requirements that require you to share your strategy with the world – all of these seem antithetical to competing effectively in the short term and to creating intrinsic value over the long term. Clearly, "going public" is good for founders and early investors to monetize their hard work in creating something with the air of durability, but beyond that, we don't see why a company would say it's better off by being public in the marketplace. We wonder whether over the next 50 years, we will see the number of public companies shrink as companies choose to go private to enable greater durability or new companies choose never to go public at all. Perhaps there might be some innovation in corporate structures that might introduce a new type of public company that doesn't have the challenges of today's version. Or maybe we will look back on this era of business and wonder why we ever thought being public was a good idea. How about you?

## MISCELLANY

Of course, we also ended up with a bunch of thoughts that were more in zygote than embryonic stage. We considered – and ultimately rejected – discussing detonating email, the proliferation of slides that permeate our meetings, and employee performance assessment, among others. We wondered about how to create greater organizational transparency, iterative thinking, and tap into the collective intelligence of an organization. But ultimately all of these ideas are best left for another day and to perhaps explore together online. But we'll end this discussion by asking you, *What would you Detonate?*

Please head online and use the hashtag #detonatethebook to weigh in. We can promise you a lively debate to unfold over time on these topics and more.

## WHAT WE HOPE YOU DO FROM HERE

Our aim with this book was not to provide you with a prescription for how to operate your business. We both strongly believe that every company situation, regardless of industry, is unique. Practices that work in one organization may not port well to another without context for how to apply them. Our goal was to give you some tangible principles to apply, without any guarantee of success. Just like the experience of baseball teams who applied analytics, smartly copying the early success of Billy Beane and the Oakland A's, keeping up with the best way of thinking about things is insufficient to be the winner. Lots of teams have applied analytics, but not all of them have won. Why? Because when everybody adopts something, the factor that makes the ultimate difference between winning and losing just moves elsewhere.

If you apply the various principles contained in this book, you'll have a better shot at winning than the average business. For the most part, most businesses still apply practices that make them susceptible to smarter competition, and our bet is that there will be more laggards than leaders when it comes to applying the *Detonate* principles. But you can't presume that others won't adopt the principles over time, so you've got to keep innovating and trying new things.

We'd encourage you to emulate Kevin Kelley – the most successful football coach you've never heard of. We are admittedly talking about American football here, a domain that might lose interest and sense in most of the world. But hopefully the broad themes of the story resonate for all, if not the specifics.

Kelley became the head football coach at Pulaski Academy in Arkansas in 2003, having previously served as the offensive coordinator for the high school from 1997 to 2002. Pulaski Academy had enjoyed moderate success over the years, but had never made it past the state championship semifinals.

Kelley declared his goal to be winning the state championship. Being mediocre wasn't acceptable. He also concluded that it was unlikely that he could expect better results while employing the same strategy as everyone else. Kelley turned to analytics to help him figure out an edge on schools that were better funded and that had stronger teams.

In his research, he came across a research paper by David Romer, an economist at the University of California at Berkeley. Romer began his research by trying to understand the degree to which best practices prevented organizations – in this case NFL franchises – from pursuing the rational, profit-maximizing course of action, an agenda near and dear to our own hearts. The paper highlighted the importance of possession in American football. It's not a complicated idea: The team that spends the most time on offense has the greatest chance of winning. That would mean that teams should pursue courses of action that – like not bunting in baseball – were typically looked down on.[59]

The research suggested unorthodox measures like "going for it" on fourth down. If a team does not successfully move the ball a certain number of yards within four "downs" of possession, they turn the ball over to the other team. There is always the option to punt – that is, offer a good hefty kick – the ball on fourth down when it comes time to turn the ball over. So most teams chose to punt the ball on fourth down to put it deep in their opponent's territory. "Going for it" – trying to make the play to achieve a first down – gave Pulaski a great chance of continuing to march down the field. But if the gambit failed, it put their opponents in great shape on the field. So, generally, it was just not done. Why? Because football coaches treated it like a rule.

But Kelley had a different idea: The Pulaski football team started violating the "rules" that everyone else followed.

They started going for it on fourth down, no matter what the situation. Pulaski also applied the principle of maintaining possession on kickoffs: Instead of kicking the ball to the other team, they attempted an onside kick (short, risky, focused on a chance to retain possession) every time. The only exception was when they were up by 21 points or more, and that was more a matter of respecting the opponent by not running up the score. To Kelley, the opportunity to gain back possession of the football through an onside kick mattered more than the risk of giving the other team an advantageous position.

Since changing philosophies, Pulaski has won seven state titles, most recently in 2017, its fourth consecutive. In 2016, *USA Today* highlighted Kelley as high school football coach of the year. Importantly, even while enjoying success, Kelley continues to try new things. Recently, he has been exploring plays that incorporate trying lateral passes and nontraditional formations.

We don't think you need to know the ins and outs of American football. But we do think that, like Kelley, you should be pursuing your own strategy, not getting stuck on what everybody else is doing. That's the essence of the message in our book.

The ossification of processes and systems into conventional wisdom permeates management as much as it does high school football or professional baseball. We're consistently amazed by situations in which someone like Kevin Kelley has been a trailblazer and shown how success is possible, but others fail to try even some elements of the strategy. Surely, there are some mediocre teams out there, say, those that have been eliminated from the playoffs that might experiment? What's the risk? What's the barrier?

Our aim with *Detonate* is to help you see beyond the constraints of best practices and to start a conversation in your organization. If you're not the executive in charge, consider asking some probing questions of your executives. If you are an executive, look around your organization for all the signs of ossification. And when you hear answers that sound like "this is the way we've always done it," zero in on those issues and demand better from your organization.

Let's light the fuse.

# NOTES

N.B. All links last accessed on December 17, 2017.

1. Zachary D. Rymer, "Explaining Why the Bunt Is Foolish in Today's MLB," *Bleacher Report*, May 14, 2013, http://bleacher report.com/articles/1639658-explaining-why-the-bunt-is-foolish -in-todays-mlb.
2. Randal S. Olson, Arend Hintze, Fred C. Dyer, David B. Knoester, and Christoph Adami, "Predator Confusion Is Sufficient to Evolve Swarming Behaviour," *Journal of the Royal Society Interface* 10, no. 85 (August 2013), http://rsif.royalsociety publishing.org/content/10/85/20130305.
3. Jim Folaron, "The Evolution of Six Sigma," *Six Sigma Forum Magazine* 2, no. 4 August 2003), http://asq.org/pub/sixsigma/past /vol2_issue4/folaron.html.
4. "After Moore's Law," *The Economist Technology Quarterly*, March 12, 2016, http://www.economist.com/technology-quarterly/2016 –03–12/after-moores-law.
5. Singularity University, "An Exponential Primer," https://su.org/ concepts/.
6. Bruce Greenwald and Steve Kahn, *Competition Demystified: A Radically Simplified Approach to Business Strategy* (New York: Portfolio, 2005).
7. Bansi Nagji and Geoff Tuff, "Managing Your Innovation Portfolio," *Harvard Business Review*, May 2012.
8. Gregory Ciotti, "Why Steve Jobs Didn't Listen to His Customers," *HuffingtonPost*, July 29, 2014, https://www.huffingtonpost .com/gregory-ciotti/why-steve-jobs-didnt-list_b_5628355.html.
9. You can read Knight's work online at http://www.econlib.org/ library/Knight/knRUP.html.
10. Cogit8R, "Who Said, 'What Gets Measured Gets Managed'?," https://athinkingperson.com/2012/12/02/who-said-what-gets-measured-gets-managed.

11. Nicole Altman, "Philadelphia's Sears Tower," *The PhillyHistory Blog*, August 7, 2014, https://www.phillyhistory.org/blog/index.php/2014/08/philadelphias-sears-tower/.

12. Poonam Kotulkar, Trupti Kshirsagar, and Aditi Vibhute, "Demolition of Structure Using Implosion Technology," *IJRITCC* 5, no. 3 (March 2017): 8–13.

13. Richard N. Foster, "Creative Disruption Whips through Corporate America," Standard & Poor's, Winter 2012; "Disruptive Forces in Europe: A Primer," *Credit Suisse Equity Research*, August 24, 2017.

14. David Pierce, "iPhone Killer: The Secret History of the Apple Watch," *Wired*, April 2015, https://www.wired.com/2015/04/the-apple-watch/.

15. Fred Lambert, "Tesla Is Going to 'Kill' the Auto Industry with Elon Musk's Way of Thinking about Manufacturing, Says SpaceX CTO," *electrek*, May 5, 2017, https://electrek.co/2017/05/15/tesla-kill-auto-industry-elon-musk-manufacturing-spacex-cto/; Dana Hull, "Tesla Says It Received More Than 325,000 Model 3 Reservations," *BloombergNews*, April 7, 2016, https://www.bloomberg.com/news/articles/2016-04-07/tesla-says-model-3-pre-orders-surge-to-325-000-in-first-week.

16. Samuel J. Palmisano, "IBM's Transformation—from Survival to Success," *Forbes*, July 7, 2010, https://www.forbes.com/2010/07/07/ibm-transformation-lessons-leadership-managing-change.html.

17. Joseph L. Bower, "Sam Palmisano's Transformation of IBM," *Harvard Business Review*, January 20, 2012, https://hbr.org/2012/01/sam-palmisanos-transformation.html.

18. Jeff Dunn, "It's Now Been 21 Straight Quarters of Declining Revenue for Tech Giant IBM," *Business Insider*, July 19, 2017, http://www.businessinsider.com/ibm-earnings-21-straight-quarters-revenue-growth-decline-chart-2017-7.

19. Make and Intel, "Maker Market Survey: An In-Depth Profile of Makers at the Forefront of Hardware Innovation," 2014; Mark Hatch, *The Maker Movement Manifesto* (New York: McGraw-Hill, 2014).

20. Deloitte, "The Maker Movement," https://www2.deloitte.com/us/en/pages/center-for-the-edge/topics/maker-movement.html.

21. A terrific collegial debate with Roger Martin and Jennifer Riel on March 17, 2015 overlooking the Manhattan skyline at the old Monitor Deloitte New York office helped inspire this thinking.
22. David Kesmodel, "Meet the Father of Zero-Based Budgeting," *Wall Street Journal*, March 26, 2015, https://www.wsj.com/articles/meet-the-father-of-zero-based-budgeting-1427415074.
23. Mark H. Freeston, Josée Rhéaume, Hélène Letarte, Michel J. Dugas, and Robert Ladouceur, "Why Do People Worry?," *Personality and Individual Differences* 17, no. 6 (December 1994): 791–802.
24. Dan W. Grupe and Jack B. Nitschke, "Uncertainty and Anticipation in Anxiety: An Integrated Neurobiological and Psychological Perspective," *Nature Reviews Neuroscience* 14, no. 7 (2013): 488–501, https://www.ncbi.nlm.nih.gov/pmc/articles/PMC4276319/.
25. Michael Pompian, *Behavioral Finance and Wealth Management: How to Build Investment Strategies That Account for Investor Biases* (Hoboken, NJ: Wiley, 2012).
26. Roger Martin, *The Design of Business* (Boston: Harvard Business Review Press, 2009).
27. AdAge Datacenter, 100 Leading National Advertisers (2011).
28. A. G. Lafley and Roger Martin, *Playing to Win: How Strategy Really Works* (Boston: Harvard Business Review Press, 2013).
29. Joana F. Cardoso and Michael R. Emes, "The Use and Value of Scenario Planning," *Modern Management Science & Engineering* 2, no. 1 (2014), www.scholink.org/ojs/index.php/mmse
30. Paul J. H. Shoemaker, "Scenario Planning: A Tool for Strategic Thinking," *Sloan Management Review*, Winter 1995, http://sloanreview.mit.edu/article/scenario-planning-a-tool-for-strategic-thinking/.
31. GBN was acquired by Monitor Group (our legacy firm), which was subsequently acquired by Deloitte.
32. Youngme Moon, *Different: Escaping the Competitive Herd* (New York: Crown Business, 2010).
33. "The Great Analytics Rankings," *ESPN*, http://www.espn.com/espn/feature/story/_/id/12331388/the-great-analytics-rankings.
34. "Major League Baseball Team Win Totals," *Baseball Reference*, https://www.baseball-reference.com/leagues/MLB/index.shtml.

35. Michael Shrage, "Tesco's Downfall Is a Warning to Data-Driven Retailers," *Harvard Business Review*, October 28, 2014, https://hbr.org/2014/10/tescos-downfall-is-a-warning-to-data-driven-retailers.

36. John Beshears, James J. Choi, David Laibson, and Brigitte C. Madrian, "How Are Preferences Revealed?" Harvard Business School and NBER White Paper, April 4, 2008, http://www.hbs.edu/faculty/Publication%20Files/how_are_preferences_revealed_79cba9af-f5ab-4ca4-b62b-6885d6e1c016.pdf.

37. Iyengar, S. S., and Lepper, M. R., "When choice is demotivating: Can one desire too much of a good thing?" *Journal of Personality and Social Psychology* 79, no. 6 (2000): 995–1006.

38. Timothy Wilson, *Strangers to Ourselves: Discovering the Adaptive Unconscious* (Cambridge: Belknap Press of Harvard University Press, 2002).

39. Paul Mercier, "Cultural Anthropology," *Encyclopedia Britannica*, https://www.britannica.com/science/cultural-anthropology.

40. "Global Revenue of Market Research from 2008 to 2016 (in Billion U.S. Dollars)," *Statista*, https://www.statista.com/statistics/242477/global-revenue-of-market-research-companies/.

41. COSO (Committee for Sponsoring Organizations of the Treadway Commission), "Enterprise Risk Management: Integrating with Strategy and Performance," June 2017.

42. Originally known as "phase gate," the practice is now mostly known as Stage-Gate, which is how we'll refer to it. https://www.stage-gate.com/aboutus_founders.php.

43. "Obama Administration Announces Columbus, OH Winner of the $40 Million Smart City Challenge to Pioneer the Future of Transportation," Press Release, https://obamawhitehouse.archives.gov/the-press-office/2016/06/23/fact-sheet-obama-administration-announces-columbus-oh-winner-40-million.

44. Richard Farson and Ralph Keyes, "The Failure-Tolerant Leader," *Harvard Business Review*, August 2002, https://hbr.org/2002/08/the-failure-tolerant-leader.

45. Cliff Kuang, "Disney's $1 Billion Bet on a Magical Wristband," *Wired*, March 10, 2015, https://www.wired.com/2015/03/disney-magicband/

46. Eyal Lanxner, "The Amazon Buy Box: How It Works for Sellers, and Why It's So Important," https://www.bigcommerce.com/blog/win-amazon-buy-box/.

47. "Nine Trends in U.S. Media Consumption: in Charts," *Media Briefing*, https://www.themediabriefing.com/article/nine-trends-in-us-media-consumption-in-charts; "Average Daily Media use in the United States from 2012 to 2018, by Device (in Minutes)," *Statista*, https://www.statista.com/statistics/270781/average-daily-media-use-in-the-us.

48. Lisa A. Robinson, W. Kip Viscusi, and Richard Zeckhauser, "Consumer Warning Labels Aren't Working," *Harvard Business Review*, November 30, 2016, https://hbr.org/2016/11/consumer-warning-labels-arent-working.

49. Jon Cohen, "New Evidence That Dengue Antibodies Trigger Life-Threatening Infections," *Science*, November 2, 2017, http://www.sciencemag.org/news/2017/11/dengue-antibodies-might-trigger-life-threatening-infections.

50. Hailey Eber, "The Rise and Fall of Blockbuster Video," *The Week*, September 24, 2010, http://theweek.com/articles/490746/rise-fall-blockbuster-video; Greg Satell, "A Look Back at Why Blockbuster Really Failed and Why It Didn't Have To," *Forbes*, September 5, 2014, https://www.forbes.com/sites/gregsatell/2014/09/05/a-look-back-at-why-blockbuster-really-failed-and-why-it-didnt-have-to/#3d4030031d64.

51. Deloitte, "Scaling Edges," https://www2.deloitte.com/us/en/pages/center-for-the-edge/articles/scaling-edges-methodology-to-create-growth.html.

52. John H. Fleming and James K. Harker, "The Next Discipline: Applying Behavioral Economics to Drive Growth and Profitability", Gallup Inc, 2013, http://www.gallup.com/file/services/178028/The%20Next%20Discipline%20-%20Applied%20Behavioral%20Economics.pdf

53. RBC Capital (http://www.businessinsider.com/amazon-presentation-by-rbc-capital-mark-mahaney-2016-12#-10).

54. Peter Cohan, "How P&G Brought Febreze Back to Life," *Telegram*, February 26, 2012, http://www.telegram.com/article/20120226/COLUMN70/102269984.

55. Richard H. Thaler and Shlomo Benartzi. "Save More Tomorrow: Using Behavioral Economics to Increase Employee Saving," *Journal of Policy Economy*, https://www.journals.uchicago.edu/doi/pdf/10.1086/380085

56. Jonathan explores this idea further in "Injecting Courage into Strategy" in the *Wall Street Journal*, March 1, 2017, http://deloitte.wsj.com/riskandcompliance/2017/03/01/injecting-courage-into-strategy/.

57. Helen Walters, Ryan Pikkel, and Brian Quinn, *The Ten Types of Innovation: The Discipline of Building Breakthroughs* (Hoboken, NJ: Wiley, 2013).

58. For cancer patients, the average survival generated by chemotherapy is 1.7 months – a figure that has been consistent since 1973. The cost of lung cancer treatment in the last year of life is $94,000 on average (http://www.newsweek.com/should-doctors-worry-about-cost-extending-life-395580). It's a sticky subject to be sure, and one that has caused a lot of controversy. We won't comment on the very personal decisions surrounding terminal illness. What we will say is that it is time to examine how we think and feel about the death of companies. As Dr. Atul Gawande said in his August 2, 2010, *New Yorker* essay "Letting Go" (https://www.newyorker.com/magazine/2010/08/02/letting-go-2), "The damage is greatest if all you do is fight to the bitter end."

59. David Romer, "Do Firms Maximize? Evidence from Professional Football," *Journal of Political Economy* 114, no. 2 (2006): 340–365.

# ACKNOWLEDGMENTS

Writing a book is one of those "learning by doing" things – you sort of know what you're in for, but it doesn't hit you until you've finished. To go from, "Hey, what do you think about writing a book?" to a finished product requires a lot of help and support. There is simply no way that *Detonate* would be in your hands – at least not in its current form and at this time – without the help of a slew of contributors.

First and foremost, we would like to thank three people who have each worked tirelessly to bring *Detonate* to life: our core team from Deloitte. Maeghan Sulham – you have done simply everything to manage this process from start to finish. Whatever we needed you to be, you were, and we are profoundly grateful for your support, encouragement, and stick-to-itiveness. Michael Anderson and Dylan Hannes – whatever quirky request we had to build out or test our ideas, you were on it. The book is better because you helped bring the ideas to life with your stories and examples. All three of you brought never-ending enthusiasm through the entire journey, and you are living proof that people thrive when they are passionate.

Tom Fishburne and Tallie Fishburne, his partner on a variety of fronts, created the cartoons found throughout the book. With their help, the pictures really have helped to make redundant thousands of words. Sarah Tuff Dunn, the writing pro among us, took our draft and edited it into something far superior.

We have also had the pleasure of learning by so many others over the years. While we can't possibly thank everyone who has influenced us over that time, we owe a debt of gratitude to those with whom we have most closely shared and debated ideas. A lot of the content in this book bears your influence, and we thank you for the ways you have impacted one or both of us. Bob Lurie, for your coaching for many, many years. You taught both of us the importance of behavioral change from day one on the job. Roger Martin, many of our ideas in *Detonate* are the direct result of our conversations and your teaching and mentorship – in strategy, of course, but also in design and the way problems should be solved. Over the years, you've challenged us whenever we offered a weak answer. We put this to good use every time we wanted to say, "Can't we just be done?" And you may still say, "Actually, you're not done." But our thinking – and this book – are better for your mentorship. Bansi Nagji, for your leadership and friendship and your ideas that helped lead us to *Detonate*. And last, but definitely not least, Jonathan Goodman. You've made this possible in so many ways, including your most helpful reviews and encouragement. Our chapter on the questions you should ask comes specifically from your teaching over the years.

There are a number of you within Deloitte who have helped make this possible with your encouragement and support: Cathy Engelbert, Jennifer Steinmann, Janet Foutty, Ambar Chowdhury, Amy Feirn, Andy Main, Tom Marriott, Jennifer Rood, Evan Hoffman, Chris Noel, Lisa Iliff, and Tony Scoles. You've all helped make this happen.

And finally, we would like to thank our spouses (respectively, not collectively) – Martha Tuff and Michelle Dunstan – and our families for putting up with us as we have shoehorned this project into our lives, mostly coming at the expense of time we'd normally spend with you. Thank you for understanding, and most of all for your unconditional support and love.

# ABOUT THE AUTHORS

Geoff Tuff is a Principal at Deloitte and a senior leader of the firm's Innovation and Applied Design practices. In the past, he led the design firm Doblin and was a senior partner at Monitor Group, serving as a member of its global Board of Directors before the company was acquired by Deloitte. He has been with some form of Monitor for more than 25 years.

Geoff's work centers on helping clients transform their businesses to grow and compete in nontraditional ways. During the course of his career, Geoff has worked in virtually every industry, and he uses that breadth of experience to bring novel insights about how things might operate to clients stuck in industry conventional wisdom.

Geoff is valued for his integrative approach to solving problems. He combines deep analytic and strategic expertise with a natural orientation toward approaches embodied in design thinking. He is a frequent speaker and writer on the topic of growth through innovation and has written for a variety of outlets, including the *Harvard Business Review*. He holds degrees from Dartmouth College and Harvard Business School.

Steven Goldbach is a Principal at Deloitte and he serves as the firm's Chief Strategy Officer. He is also a member of the Deloitte U.S. Executive Leadership Team. Prior to joining Deloitte, Steve was a partner at Monitor Group and head of its New York office.

Steve helps executives and their teams transform their organizations by making challenging and pragmatic strategy choices in the face of uncertainty. He is an architect, expert practitioner, and teacher of the variety of strategy methodologies developed and used by Monitor Deloitte over the years. Serving clients in many industries, including consumer products, telecommunications, media, and health care, Steve helps companies combine rigor and creativity to create their own future.

Previously, Steve was the Director of Strategy at Forbes. He holds degrees from Queen's University at Kingston and Columbia Business School.

# INDEX